19-15

French Chansons of the Sixteenth Century

French Chansons
of the Sixteenth Century

Edited by
Jane A. Bernstein

The Pennsylvania State University Press
University Park and London

For my mother and father
Claire and Samuel Bernstein
With love and gratitude

Library of Congress Cataloging in Publication Data
Main entry under title:

French chansons of the sixteenth century.

French words with English translations.
Bibliography: p. 211
1. Chansons, Polyphonic — 16th century.
I. Bernstein, Jane A.
M1579.F73   1985   84-43062
ISBN 0-271-00397-9

Contents

Contents

Preface

The advent of music printing in the sixteenth century generated new life in the French polyphonic chanson, a musical form that had existed for over two centuries. From the presses in Paris, Lyons, Venice, Nuremburg, Louvain, Antwerp, and for a brief time, London, thousands of chansons were disseminated throughout Europe. The favored form these new musical publications took was the *recueil*, a collection of chansons written by several composers. Although the anthology had always been the plan for musical manuscripts of previous centuries, the *recueil* proved a highly marketable publication aimed at a wide musical audience that included not only the wealthy aristocracy but also a burgeoning middle-class.

"Something for everyone" might have been the sixteenth-century publisher's motto, for here the elegant courtly love song (*chanson courtois*) appeared alongside the obscene narrative (*chanson grivoise*), drinking song and dance tune. Highly contrapuntal paraphrase chansons were juxtaposed with simple *voix de villes* or devout *chansons spirituelles*.

The present anthology imitates its sixteenth-century counterpart by presenting a compendium of chansons from all the main musical centers of Europe. Intended for both the amateur and professional musician as well as the music scholar, it has been arranged for a variety of uses. Each chanson forms a complete unit containing musical setting, full poetic text and English translation, historical description, and brief critical commentary listing original sources, modern editions, emendations, and textual sources. The performer may therefore extract one chanson without having to refer to any other part of the anthology.

Chansons can also be joined together into larger groupings for performance programs or for study purposes. Different musical settings of a single chanson poem, as in the case of Clément Marot's *Jouissance vous donneray* (Nos. 1, 12, 16, and 17), or the musical style of composers from a particular geographic area like the Low Countries (Nos. 13–21, 23–30, and 35) could be examined, or a specific chanson genre such as the bawdy song (*chanson grivoise*), (Nos. 4, 6, 14, 15, 19, 20, 22, and 30) might be studied.

Lastly, the anthology followed from beginning to end presents a concise history of the sixteenth-century chanson—a valuable guide for the music student interested in exploring the various musical styles of the French chanson. Of all the chansons represented in this edition, only one type has been omitted, that in *musique mesurée*. *Musique mesurée à l'antique*, as it was more commonly known, was the setting to music of French verse that followed the quantitative principles of Greek and Latin poetry (i.e., *vers mesurés*). This type of chanson belongs more to the history of the solo song or *air de cour* than of the polyphonic chanson.

The performer and student wishing to delve deeper into the history of the sixteenth-century chanson will discover a wealth of literary material. Here are but a few of the more recent works available in English:

General Sources: Howard Brown, *Music in the Renaissance* (Englewood Cliffs, N.J.: 1976), chapters 7, 8, 11; Isabelle Cazeaux, *French Music of the Fifteenth and Sixteenth Centuries* (Oxford: 1975); Daniel Heartz, "The Chanson in the Humanist Era" in *Current Thought in Musicology*, ed. John Grubbs (Austin, Texas: 1976), pp. 193–230; François Lesure, *Musicians and Poets of the French Renaissance* (New York: 1955); Gustave Reese, *Music in the Renaissance*, rev. ed. (New York: 1959), chapters 6 and 8.

Detailed Studies: Lawrence Bernstein, "The 'Parisian Chanson': Problems of Style and Terminology," *Journal of the American Musicological Society*, Vol. XXXI (1978), 193–240; Lawrence Bernstein, "*La Courone et fleur des chansons a troys*—A Mirror of the French Chanson in Italy in the Years between Ottaviano Petrucci and Antonio Gardane," *Journal of the American Musicological Society*, Vol. XXIV (1973), 3–68; Howard Brown, *Music in the French Secular Theater 1400–1550* (Cambridge, Mass.: 1963); Howard Brown, "The *Chanson rustique*: Popular Elements in the 15th and 16th Century Chanson," *Journal of the American Musicological Society*, Vol. XII (1959), 16–26; James Haar, ed., *Chanson and Madrigal: 1480–1530* (Cambridge, Mass.: 1964); Daniel Heartz, *Pierre Attaingnant, Royal Printer of Music* (Berkeley, Calif.: 1969); Daniel Heartz, "*Voix de ville*: Between Humanist Ideals and Musical Realities" in *Words and Music: The Scholar's View, A Medley of Problems and Solutions Compiled in Honor of A. Tillman Merritt by Sundry Hands*, ed. Laurence Berman (Cambridge, Mass.: 1972), 115–35; Kenneth Levy, "*Susanne un jour*: The History of a 16th Century Chanson," *Annales musicologiques*, III (1955), 213–63.

In addition to these literary sources, there are three modern anthologies of chansons which deal with a specific geographical location or a particular genre: Howard Brown, ed., *Theatrical Chansons of the Fifteenth and Early Sixteenth Centuries* (Cambridge, Mass.: 1963); François Lesure, ed., *Anthologie de Chanson Parisienne au XVIe siècle* (Monaco: 1953); Albert Seay, ed., *Thirty Chansons for Three and Four Voices from Attaingnant's Collections*, *Collegium musicum*, I/2 (New Haven, Conn.: 1960).

My thanks to the staffs at the British Library, Christ Church College Library, Oxford, the Paris Bibliothèque Nationale, the Music Library of the University of California, Berkeley, and the Isham Library, Harvard University. To the Tufts University Faculty Awards Committee and Vassar College I am grateful for grants which aided in the completion of this project. I am indebted to Howard Batchelor and Alan Clayton for their help with English translations, and to Daniel Heartz, Philip Brett, Lawrence Bernstein, and Isabelle Cazeaux for valuable suggestions and information they supplied. I owe a special debt of gratitude to my friend, Craig Monson, who was kind enough to read the entire commentary of this anthology. Lastly, I wish to thank my husband, James Ladewig, for his constant support and encouragement throughout this project.

Editorial Methods

Only original clefs are given at the beginning of each piece, since original pitch, time signature, and key signature have been retained. All note values have been halved *with the exception* of Nos. 28, 30, and 34, in which original note values have been preserved. The range of each vocal part appears after modern signatures. Ligatures are indicated by brackets above the staff. Original accidentals appear before the note and remain valid for the whole bar unless cancelled. Editorial accidentals dealing with *musica ficta* are placed above the staff and affect only the note below. Cancellatory and cautionary accidentals appear in parentheses before the note. The text underlay has been taken from the superius partbook of the earliest printed musical source. Except for obvious errors, original spellings have been retained. Following Brian Jeffrey, *Chanson Verse of the Early Renaissance,* vols. I and II (London: 1971 and 1976), a distinction has been made between *u* and *v, i* and *j*; accents have been added on à, là, où, and é as well as cedillas wherever necessary. Punctuation and capitalization of line beginnings have been modernized, and elisions employed. In addition, numbering of stanzas, indentation, and indication of refrains have also been utilized in the poetic texts that appear after the musical settings. All text underlay in brackets has been supplied by the editor.

Note about the Critical Commentary

SOURCES

These include extant musical publications of the sixteenth century. Musical manuscripts are also cited when they are a unique or important source. Except where noted, the earliest music publication is used as the main source for this edition. The dates of RISM (*International Inventory of Musical Sources. Recueils imprimés XVIe–XVIIe siècles*, ed. François Lesure, Vol. I [Munich-Duisberg: 1960]), and Brown (Howard Brown, *Instrumental Music Printed Before 1600; A Bibliography* [Cambridge, Mass.: 1965]) are used as abbreviations for the full titles of sixteenth-century publications. Titles, publishers, and publication dates for all printed sources may be found in the bibliography of original sources at the end of the book.

MODERN EDITIONS

About one-half of the chansons in this anthology appear in other modern editions. Some of these are out-of-print; most are in scholarly complete works of individual composers. Complete citations for all of these editions occur in this section.

EMENDATIONS

Corrections of text and notes supplied by the editor are indicated here.

TEXT

The author, earliest surviving literary publication, and modern edition of the chanson verse appear in this section. Bracketed stanzas indicate that they are found only in literary sources.

1. Joyssance vous donneray

[Clément Marot]

Claudin de Sermisy

Joyssance vous donneray,
Mon amy, et vous meneray
Là où pretend vostre esperance.
Vivante ne vous laisseray;
Encor quant morte je seray
L'esprit en aura souvenance.

[Si pour moy avez du soucy,
Pour vous n'en ay pas moins aussi,
Amour le vous doit faire entendre.
Mais s'il vous griefve d'estre ainsi,
Appaisez vostre cueur transi.
Tout vient à point qui peult attendre.]

Fulfillment will I give you, my beloved, and I will lead you where your hope aspires. While I live, I will never leave you, and even in death, my spirit will always remember.

[If my care for you is no less than yours for me, love should teach you this. But since it troubles you, ease your tormented heart. All things come to those who wait.]

On 4 April 1528, the first French publication of polyphonic music, *Chansons nouvelles musique à quatres parties*, issued from the press of Pierre Attaingnant. This collection, which simply promised "new songs," in fact proffered to the musical world a totally different kind of chanson—the so-called Parisian chanson.

Among the first and foremost composers of this new chanson was Claudin de Sermisy. Born around 1490, Claudin is first mentioned in 1508 as a cleric at the Sainte Chapelle; from there he moved to the Chapelle Royale, where he was a singer at the court of Louis XII. Under Francis I, Claudin became its musical director, the most prestigious post in all of France. Because his works dominated the early publications of the Royal printer, Attaingnant, Claudin's name became synonymous with the *chanson parisienne.*

It was during this time that another artist at the court of Francis I, a young poet named Clément Marot, sought to change the traditional forms of French poetry. In giving up the rigid rules of the Rhétoriqueur, Marot adopted a poetic style similar to that of popular and folk texts. Abandoning the complicated, repetitive schemes of the rondeau, ballade, and virelai, Marot simplified the poetic structure by substituting a four- to ten-line stanza of eight or ten syllables per line. This introduction of the popular into the courtly world can be observed in Marot's poem, *Joyssance vous donneray,* where an ease of expression and direct simplicity instill new life into the traditional theme of courtly love.

Claudin de Sermisy was the first composer to set Marot's texts, and Pierre Attaingnant printed several in his inaugural publication, including the most celebrated of them, *Joyssance vous donneray.* This popular chanson was not only reprinted in numerous publications and copied into manuscripts that were spread throughout the Continent and even to England, but was also arranged for a variety of instruments. Its tenor part became a basse dance tune that appeared in dance treatises such as the famous *Orchesographie* by Thoinot Arbeau. It was used as a model for chansons by other composers (three of which are included in this anthology, nos. 12, 16, and 17 below), and representations of the musical score of *Joyssance vous donneray* are even portrayed in a few sixteenth-century French paintings.

Claudin's chanson exemplifies the new French style. Written in a clear, homo-rhythmic idiom, it opens with the familiar dactylic rhythmic pattern (long, short, short) of the Parisian chanson. The phrases alternate between a chordal and a simple imitative texture. The musical form of the chanson closely adheres to the poetic scheme:

Music: A B C B (B)
Text: aa b aa b (b)

Most important though, the melodic interest in the Parisian chanson shifts from the tenor part to the top voice. Curiously, the tenor of *Joyssance vous donneray* maintains its own melodic independence. Its text differs from the other parts at the last line of the poem (*Si vous auray en souvenance*), and the repetition of its second musical phrase for the fifth line forms an even closer relationship with the poetic structure than that of the superius line. These characteristics strongly suggest that unlike the tenor of most Parisian chansons, this one was conceived before the superius.

SOURCES: RISM: 1528[3] f. 7v, [c. 1528][8] f. 5 (re-ed: 1531[2] f. 6), 1536[2] f. 7v; Brown: 1529[3], 1531[3], 1546[18], 1589[1]. Cambrai, Bibl. de la Ville, MS 125–128, f. 138v; Danzig, Stadtbibl., MS 4003, Bk. 1, no. 57; Florence, Bibl. Naz. Centr., MS XIX, 111, f. 1; Florence, Bibl. Naz. Centr., MS XIX, 112, f. 6; Basel, Univ. Bibl., MS F. IX. 59–62, no. 44; Basel, Univ. Bibl., MS F. X. 17–20, no. 71; London, Royal College of Music, MS 1070, p. 26; Munich, Bayer. Staatsbibl. Mus. MS 1501, no. 6; Copenhagen, Kgl. Bibl., MS Ny Kgl. S. 1848, pp. 182 and 210; Regensburg, Proske Bibl. MS A.R. 940/41, no. 104; Vienna, Oesterreichische Nat. Bibl. MS 18110, no. 21.

MODERN EDITIONS: Isabelle Cazeaux, ed., *Claudin de Sermisy, Collected Works, Corpus Mensurabilis Musicae* 52 (1974), III, p. 138. Albert Seay, ed., *Pierre Attaingnant, Transcriptions of Chansons for Keyboard, Corpus Mensurabilis Musicae* 20 (1961), p. 192.

EMENDATIONS: Tenor, bars 17–18, f′ not tied in RISM 1528[3] but is in subsequent editions.

TEXT: Clément Marot, *L'Adolescence Clementine* (1532), modern edition in C. A. Mayer, ed., *Clément Marot, Oeuvres Lyriques* (London: 1964), p. 177. The second stanza of the poem does not appear in any of the musical sources.

2. O combien est malheureux le desir

Claudin de Sermisy

O com- bien est mal-heu-reux le de- sir Dont
De mon en- nuy j'ay for-mé ung plai- sir Qui

O com- bien est mal- heu-reux le de- sir
De mon en- nuy j'ay for- mé ung plai- sir

O com- bien est mal- heu-reux le de- sir
De mon en- nuy j'ay for- mé ung plai- sir

O com- bien est mal- heu-reux le de- sir
De mon en- nuy j'ay for- mé ung plai-sir

je ne puis re- cep- voir que tour - - - ment!
est trop loing de mon con-ten - - te

Dont je ne puis re- cep- voir que tour - ment!
Qui est trop loing de mon con- ten-te

Dont je ne puis re-cep - voir que tour - ment!
Qui est trop loing de mon con - ten- te

Dont je ne puis re-cep - voir que tour - ment!
Qui est trop loing de mon con - ten - te

-ment. Je voy mon bien fi - nir soub-dai-ne-ment; Mon tra-vail croict soubz
-ment. Je voy mon bien fi - nir soub-dai - ne - ment; Mon tra - vail croict
-ment. Je voy mon bien fi - nir soub-dai-ne - ment; Mon tra-vail croict
-ment. Je voy mon bien fi - nir soub-dai - ne - ment; Mon tra-vail croict

O combien est malheureux le desir

O combien est malheureux le desir
Dont je ne puis recepvoir que tourment!
De mon ennuy j'ay formé ung plaisir
Qui est trop loing de mon contentement.
Je voy mon bien finir soubdainement;
Mon travail croict soubz couverte pensée.
Sans esperer, je seuffre doulcement
Le mal que sent une amye offencée.

How wretched is that love from which nothing but torment springs! Although I have made a pleasure from my grief, it is far from contentment. I see my reward suddenly disappear, while my pain deep inside increases. Hopeless, I meekly suffer the pangs of a rejected love.

Claudin's elegant miniature, "O combien est malheureux le desir," displays the simple texture and compact proportions associated with the new Parisian style. The repetition of phrases at the opening and at the end (A A B C A A) often occurs in the chansons printed by Attaingnant, as does the shift of the main melodic line from the tenor to the top voice. But certain subtleties of Claudin's own style in this chanson set him apart from his lesser contemporaries. The close musical correspondence to the poetic scheme as seen in the first four lines:

Music: A A
Text: ab ab

and the symmetrical construction of the phrases (in ten bar groupings) appear frequently in Claudin's vocal works. But it is the composer's infallible sense of line that remains the hallmark of his style. The graceful, seemingly endless melody in the superius, the lyrical quality of the tenor part which moves in thirds and sixths with the superius, and the smooth voice leading in the bass and contratenor betray the work of a master of the genre.

SOURCES: *Onziesme livre contenant xxviii chansons . . .* (Attaingnant: 1541) f. 5v (re-ed: RISM 1542^{14} f. 5v, 1542^{15} f. 5v), 1544^{12} f. 15v, 1550^6 f. 1v, 1550^8 f. 1v, 1560^6 p. 31 (re-ed: 1562^3 p. 4 [attrib. to Sandrin], 1570^8 p. 4, 1573^4 f. 21, 1576^{2a} f. 21, 1589^5 f. 29, 1592^8 f. 21, 1597^9 f. 21, 1601^4 f. 21, 1605^5 f. 21, 1608^{11} f. 21, 1609^{12} f. 21, 1613^7 f. 21, 1617^{6-6a} f. 21, 1632^5 f. 21, 1633^2 f. 21, 1640^6 f. 21, 1644^3 f. 21); *Tiers livre du Recueil . . .* (Du Chemin: 1561), f. 1v; Brown: 1546_{18}, 1549_8, 1552_{11}, 1553_1, 1562_3, 1563_{12}, 1568_6, 1568_7, 1570_3, 1571_6, 1578_4; The Hague, Koninklijke Bibl., MS 74.H.7, f. 35; Vienna, Oesterreichische Nat. Bibl., MS 18811, f. 41; Winchester, Winc. College Lib., 16th cent. ptbks, f. 93; York, Yorkminster Lib. M.91.(S), f. 99.

MODERN EDITIONS: Isabelle Cazeaux, ed., *Claudin de Sermisy, Collected Works, Corpus Mensurabilis Musicae 52* (1974), IV, p. 35. K. Ph. Bernet Kempers, *Jacobus Clemens non Papa, Collected Works, Corpus Mensurabilis Musicae 4* (1959), VII, p. 156.

TEXT: Anonymous, *La fleur de poesie françoyse . . .* (Lotrian: 1543). Two responses of "Le mal que sent une amye offencée" appear in the sixteenth century, one by Dutertre in RISM 1547^{12} and the other anonymously in 1560^6 and in subsequent editions of this publication.

3. Vivre ne puis content sans ma maistresse

Pierre Certon

Vivre ne puis content sans ma maistresse

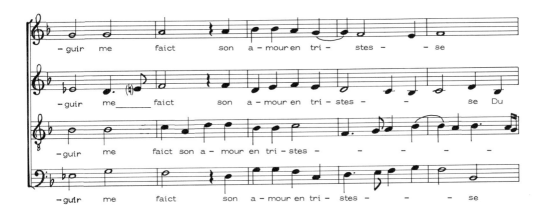

23

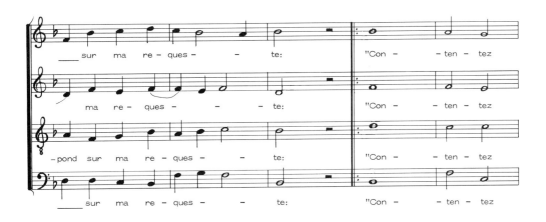

Vivre ne puis content sans ma maistresse,
Son doulx regard incessament regrette.
Languir me faict son amour en tristesse
Du quel elle a congnoyssance parfaicte.
Joyssance est le bien que souhaite
Pour avoir fruict de l'amour commencée.
Mais en chantant, respond sur ma requeste:
"Contentez vous, amy, de la pensée!"

I cannot live happily without my love; her sweet look I constantly miss. None could know better than she that I languish in sadness for her love. Pleasure is the thing that I desire; I wish to reap the fruit of this budding love. But in singing she answers my plea: "Content yourself, my friend, with the thought!"

As Master of the Children at the Sainte Chapelle, Pierre Certon played a vital role in the musical life of the French court. His works, next to Claudin's, were the most frequently published in Paris, and after the death of Attaingnant, they retained their popularity with the younger generation of publishers.

Certon was in fact the friend of Claudin de Sermisy, "the great scholar among musicians and great friend of scholars," as Certon addresses the older composer in a dedication to a volume of his own motets in 1542. And in 1562 after Claudin's death, Certon composed a deploration honoring his former associate.

"Vivre ne puis content sans ma maistresse" also pays homage to Certon's friend by including in its superius quotations from three different chansons by Claudin: "Vivre ne puis content sans sa presence," "Languir me fais sans t'avoir offensé," and "Contentez vous, amy, de la pensée." While only the opening four notes (as well as the words) of the first two Claudin chansons are used, the melody of the entire first line of "Contentez vous, amy, de la pensée" appears intact at the end of the Certon setting. This chanson is not a parody or paraphrase work, however, since it does not elaborate or develop the borrowed material. It can best be compared to the *fricassée*, in which many different chansons are quoted in quodlibet fashion.

SOURCES: RISM 1538[14] f. 2v, 1540[12] f. 3v, 1540[16] f. 29, 1544[12] f. 9.

MODERN EDITION: H. Expert and A. Agnel, eds., *Maîtres anciens de la musique française*, II, *Pierre Certon* (Paris: 1967), p. 74.

TEXT: Anonymous, *La fleur de poesie françoyse . . .* (Lotrian: 1543).

4. Frere Thibault, sejourné gros et gras

[Clément Marot]

Pierre Certon

Frere Thibault, Frere Thibault, se-jour-né gros et

Frere Thibault, Frere Thibault, se-jour-né gros et

Frere Thibault, Frere Thibault, se-jour-né gros et

Frere Thibault, Frere Thibault, se-jour-né gros et

gras, Ti- roit de nuyt u-ne gar-se en che-mi - - - se

gras, Ti-roit de nuyt, ti-roit de nuyt u-ne gar-se en che-mi - se Par le treil-lis

gras, Ti-roit de nuyt u-ne gar-se en che-mi - se Par le treil-

gras, Ti-roit de nuyt, ti-roit de nuyt u-ne gar-se en che-mi - se

Par le treil-lis, par le treil-lis de sa cham-bre où les bras El -

par le treil-lis par le treil-lis de sa cham-bre où les bras El - le pas -

- lis, par le treil-lis de sa cham-bre où les bras

Par le treil-lis, par le treil - lis de sa cham-bre où les bras El - le pas -

Frere Thibault, sejourné gros et gras

Frere Thibault, sejourné gros et gras,
Tiroit de nuyt une garse en chemise
Par le treillis de sa chambre, où les bras
Elle passa, puis la teste y a mise,
Et puis le seing, mais elle fut bien prise,
Car le fessier y passer ne peult onc.
"Par la mort bieu," ce dict le moyne adonc,
"Il ne m'en chault de bras, tetin ne teste;
Passez le cul, ou vous retirez donc,
Je ne sçauroys sans luy vous faire feste."

Idle Brother Thibault, fat and well-oiled, was hauling a wench in her smock through the bars of his chamber-window; when arms, head, bosom, and all had passed, she got quite stuck at her backside. "For God's sake," said the monk. "What the hell's the use of head, arms and tits? Put your ass through, or get out, for without it, I can't delight you."

Frere Thibault of this anticlerical epigram by Clément Marot represents a favorite character of the fabliau and other popular literature of the Middle Ages and Renaissance—the lecherous monk. Of Marot's poems, the epigram proved the most popular among chanson composers, who set around fifty of them to music. The later humanist poet, Joachim Du Bellay, defined the epigram as "a type of work which is under no obligation to say anything of consequence in its initial nine lines provided the tenth line supplies the reader with some tenuous witticism provoking laughter."

Pierre Certon set this licentious narrative in the syllabic, declamatory style of the Parisian chanson. Note the skillful contrast in texture between the light imitative opening and the dance-like chordal section in triple time. Another French composer, Clément Janequin, wrote an equally amusing chanson upon this same epigram.

SOURCES: RISM: 1538[13] f. 1v (re-ed: 1540[11], f. 1v), 1538[17] f. 7, 1549[18] f. 2v, 1549[28] f. 4 (re-ed: 1551[6] f. 4).

MODERN EDITION: H. Expert and A. Agnel, eds., *Maîtres anciens de la musique française*, II, *Pierre Certon* (Paris: 1967), p. 66.

TEXT: *Les Oeuvres de Clément Marot* (E. Dolet, Lyon: 1538); modern edition: *Clément Marot: Épigrammes*, ed. C. A. Mayer (London: 1970), p. 133.

5. O mal d'aymer qui tous maulx oultrepasse

Clément Janequin

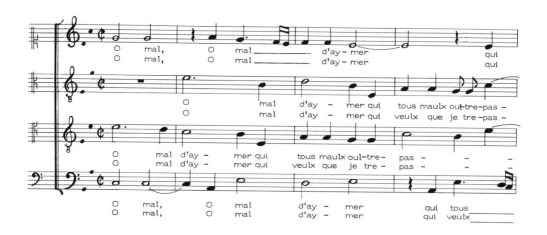

O mal d'aymer qui tous maulx oultrepasse,
O mal d'aymer qui les hommes martyre,
O mal d'aymer qui veulx que je trepasse,
O mal qui fais que mon las cueur empire,
Or sus, tous maulx, esponge qui attire
Complainctes, pleurs, ennuys, gemissementz,
O mal qui n'as devant ny apres pire,
Un jour sois las de me livrer torment.

Oh pain of love, all woes surpassing, pain of love who martyrs men and wishes me dead, oh grief that weighs heavy on my tired heart. Be gone all ills, source of laments, tears, griefs, groans. Oh sickness which surpasses all others may you one day be weary of tormenting me.

The third leading figure of the Parisian chanson was Clément Janequin. Unlike his contemporaries Claudin and Certon, Janequin spent a good portion of his life in Bordeaux and then in Angers before he moved to Paris in 1549. Many of his chansons appeared in print during his stay at Angers, where he held a post at the Cathedral until 1537. A total of 263 chansons have survived—a body of works much larger than any other composer of the sixteenth century.

Janequin is best known for his programmatic chansons, where he imitates sounds of birds, the hunt, and the street. His most famous onomatopoeic work, *La bataille*, probably commemorates the Battle of Marignano. In addition to the programmatic chanson, Janequin excelled in several other chanson styles in both the popular and the courtly vein. "O mal d'aymer qui tous maulx oultrepasse" represents the serious side of courtly love.

Parisian chansons in this solemn style tend to avoid extreme expression of the text. Unlike the Italian madrigal where words such as "death," "tears," and "pain" elicit a musical response, the French chanson offers a more restrained setting of its poem. French composers concentrate instead upon the rhythmic aspects of the text rather than coloring the words through harmony and chromaticism. Individual words in the chanson are often glossed over, while the general comprehension of the text is emphasized through a declamatory, syllabic setting. Occasionally though, a Parisian chanson does contain "madrigalisms," as in this exceptional work by Janequin. Here the repetition of the opening words *O mal*, marked off with rests in the top voice, suggests the Italianate style that, as we shall see, played a decisive role in the French chanson of the late sixteenth century.

SOURCES: RISM: 1544[7] f. 5v (re-ed: 1544[8] f. 12v); *Second livre du Recueil . . .* (Du Chemin: 1561) f. 9v.

MODERN EDITION: A. Tillman Merritt and François Lesure, eds., *Clément Janequin, Chansons polyphoniques* (Monaco: 1967), III, p. 128.

TEXT: Anonymous, "Du mal d'aymer qui tous maulx outrepasse" in *La Recreation et passetemps des tristes pour resjouyr les melencoliques . . .* (L'Huillier: 1573).

6. Or vien ça, vien, m'amye Perrette

Clément Janequin

Or vien ça, vien, m'amye Perrette

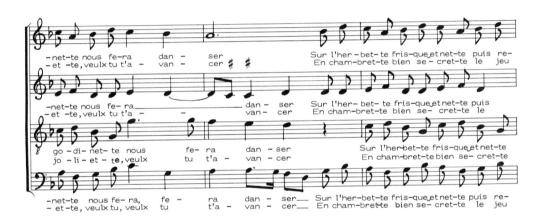

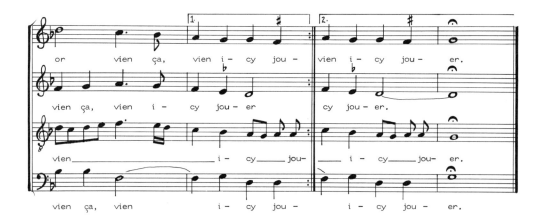

Or vien ça, vien, m'amye Perrette,
Or vien ça, vien icy jouer.
Ton cul servira de tron, de trompette,
Et ton devant fera la feste.
Si te plaist de nous le louer
De ce je n'en veulx mye
Et en jour de ma vie
Je n'y voulu penser.
    Or vien ça, vien, m'amye [Perrette],
    Or vien ça, vien icy jouer.
Ta musette godinette nous fera danser
Sur l'herbette frisque et nette puis recon, puis recommancer.

    Or vien ça, vien, m'amye Perrette,
    Or vien ça, vien icy jouer.
Nous dirons une chanson, une chansonnette,
Et sur la plaisante brunette
Noz deux corps irons esprouver.
J'en ay si grant envye
Qu'à peu que ne desvie.
Plus ne m'y fault penser.
    Or vien ça, vien, m'amye [Perrette],
    Or vien ça, vien icy jouer.
Mignonnette, jolyette, veulx tu t'avancer
En chambrette bien secrette le jeu con, le jeu commancer?
    Or vien ça, vien, m'amye Perrette,
    Or vien ça, vien icy jouer.

Now come, oh come, Perrette my love; come, oh come here to play. Your ass will make a trum—, trumpet. And what's up front will make us glad. If you wish to lend it to us all, then I will have no part, nor in all of my life did I have this in mind. Now then come, oh come my friend, come here to play. Your pretty little bagpipe will make us dance on the fresh and sweet grass. So let's, come, come begin again.

Now come, oh come, Perrette my love; come, oh come here to play. We will sing a pretty little canzonet about the pleasant brunette and on the grass our two bodies will be one. I want to do it so much that I am almost going crazy. I should no longer think of it. Now come, oh come, my love, come here to play. Dear one, pretty one, won't you come with me in the secret room to cont—, continue the game?

In addition to the programmatic and courtly chansons, Janequin cultivated the light-hearted licentious chanson. In these *chansons grivoises*, the carefree existence of country life comes alive. Peasants and shepherdesses with names like Perrette, Robin, Marion, Jacquet, and Margot inhabit this rustic world, where obscene puns and erotic imagery (e.g., the trumpets, bagpipes, and other such "instruments" of "Or vien ça, vien, m'amye Perrette") abound.

Janequin turned these vulgar little poems into rhythmic *tours de force*, an effect achieved by the rapid declamation of long and involved texts, restriction of the vocal ranges, and persistent reiteration of single pitches.

Although "Or vien ça, vien, m'amye Perrette" is not, strictly speaking, a programmatic chanson, it is full of descriptive effects. Janequin, for example, imitates the trumpet by continually repeating the interval of a fifth in the bass part (bars 10–11 and 13–15), and the drone of the bagpipe can be heard in the superius and bass (bars 32–33).

SOURCES: RISM: 1536^6 f. 1v, 1540^{17} f. 7; Brown: 1533_2, 1553_1, 1554_6, 1560_3, 1562_{10}, 1564_1, 1568_7, 1574_7, 1591_3.

MODERN EDITION: A. Tillman Merritt and François Lesure, eds., *Clément Janequin, Chansons polyphoniques* (Monaco: 1965), II, p. 82.

TEXT: Anonymous, *La Recreation et passetemps des tristes pour resjouyr les melencoliques* . . . (L'Huillier: 1573).

7. Au joly son du sansonnet

Passereau

Au joly son du sansonnet

Au joly son du sansonnet

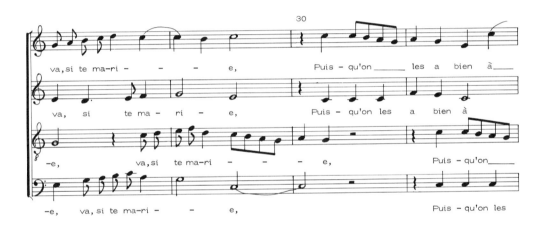

Au joly son du sansonnet
Je m'endormy l'autre nuyctée,
Et là ouy dire ung souhait
Qui touchoit à m'amye:
    "Va, si te marie,
Puisqu'on les a bien à l'essay,
Jamays je ne me mariray."

To the starling's sweet voice I fell asleep last night. Its song expressed a wish about my sweet-heart: "Go on," it said, "Get married if you want to, but since there are plenty of women to be had without trying, I myself, shall never marry."

Little is known about the life of Passereau. In 1509 he was listed as a tenor in the Chapel of the Duke of Angoulême, who became Francis I, King of France, some six years later. Perhaps Passereau remained in the service of the king, or at least lived in the French capital, as twenty-four of his works were printed by the Parisian publisher, Attaingnant. Evidence of the composer's widespread fame appears in an account by the sixteenth-century Italian actor and playwright, Andrea Calmo, who heard Passereau's chanson "Il est bel et bon" sung in the streets of Venice.

Like "Il est bel et bon," "Au joly son du sansonnet" illustrates the light, "rustic" chanson style in which Passereau excelled. The close imitation, quick syllabic declamation, and running melodic figures are all features of Passereau's style.

SOURCES: RISM: 1536[4] f. 28v, 1538[10] f. 14 (re-ed: 1546[11] f. 14).

MODERN EDITIONS: Georges Dottin, ed., *Passereau, Collected Works, Corpus Mensurabilis Musicae* 45 (1967), p. 44.

TEXT: Anonymous, *La fleur de poesie françoyse* . . . (Lotrian: 1543).

8. Grace, vertu, bonté, beaulté, noblesse

Roquelay

Grace, vertu, bonté, beaulté, noblesse
Sont à m'amye; point ne le fault celer.
Trop my desplaist d'en ouyr mal parler;
Je hay celuy qui son honneur blesse.

Grace, virtue, goodness, beauty, nobility, my beloved possesses them all. This should in no way be hidden. Much it displeases me to hear evil spoken of her; I despise him who wounds her honor.

Many of the Parisian chanson texts contained decasyllabic lines, frequently with a break or caesura after the fourth syllable. Time and again, the opening phrase began with a dactylic pattern (long, short, short) on the same pitch. The resulting rhythmic formula became a trademark not only of the Parisian chanson, but also of its instrumental successor, the Italian *canzona*.

"Grace, vertu, bonté, beaulté, noblesse" displays this stylized rhythmic pattern as well as the clear chordal texture and repetition of the last phrase common to the *chanson parisienne*. Of its composer, Roquelay, nothing is known. He was probably of

French origin, since his five extant works were published by Attaingnant from 1529 to 1537. "Grace, vertu, bonté, beaulté, noblesse," his most popular chanson, also appeared in various lute publications and was arranged in two- and three-part settings by the composer-publishers, Antoine Gardane and Tylman Susato. Certon, Nicolas, and Heurteur utilized this quatrain as well for their own polyphonic settings.

SOURCES: RISM: [1528]^5 f. 5, 1536^3 f. 12v, 1537^3 f. 6v; Brown: 1547$_7$, 1552$_{11}$, 1563$_{12}$; London, British Lib., Royal Appendix MSS 56 and 58, f. 20, f. 30v; Cambrai, Bibl. de la Ville MS 125–128, f. 34; Florence, Bibl. Medicea-Laurenziana MS Ashburnham 1085, f. 34; Paris, Bibl. nat. MS Rés 255, f. 34, Ulm, Dombibl. MS 237, f. 84.

9. Le rossignol plaisant et gracieulx

Mittantier

Le rossignol plaisant et gracieulx
Habiter veult tousjours au vert boccaige,
Aux champs voler et par tous aultres lieux,
Sa liberté aymant plus que la caige.
Mais le mien cueur, qui demeure en hostaige
Soubz triste deuil, qui le tient en ses las,
Du rossignol ne cherche l'advantaige,
Ne de son chant recepvoir le soulas.

The nightingale so pleasant and so gay,
In greenwood groves delights to make his dwelling.
In fields to fly, chanting his roundelay,
At liberty, against the cage rebelling.
But my poor heart, with sorrows over-swelling,
Through bondage vile, binding my freedom short,
No pleasure takes in these his sports excelling,
Nor in his song receiveth no comfort.

The nightingale is a common motif that runs through the medieval love-lyric. Often the name of Philomela, the Athenian princess who, according to Classical mythology, was transformed into a nightingale, would appear interchangeably with that of the nightingale in these poems.

By the fourteenth century, imitations of the nightingale's mellifluous song along with other bird calls occurred in the onomatopoeic virelai. The literary theme of the nightingale continued to remain fashionable through the sixteenth century in the courtly chanson, where its sweet song might soothe the troubled heart of a suffering lover, or as a caged bird symbolize an imprisoned love.

Mittantier's "Le rossignol plaisant et gracieulx," in the typical Parisian chanson style, is the earliest musical setting of this, the best known of the nightingale chansons. The text inspired no fewer than eight composers to set it to music, among them, Certon, Le Blanc, Millot, Castro, Pevernage, Lassus, Ferrabosco, and even the Englishman, William Byrd. The Lassus version, by far the most famous, was printed many times in Paris. It later made its way across the channel into an anthology mainly devoted to Italian madrigals: Nicholas Yonge's *Musica Transalpina* of 1588. The charming translation presented here comes from this English source.

SOURCES: RISM: 1539[15] f. 12v (re-ed: 1539[16] f. 12v), 1540[17] f. 19.

MODERN EDITION: Albert Seay, ed., *Mittantier and Vassal, Collected Chansons, Corpus Mensurabilis Musicae* 66 (1974), p. 44.

TEXT: Anonymous, *La fleur de poesie françoyse . . .* (Lotrian: 1543).

10. Sy mon travail vous peult donner plaisir

Sandrin

Sy mon travail vous peult donner plaisir
Recepvant d'autre plus de contentement,
Ne creignez plus me faire desplaisir
Et en laissez à mes yeulx le tourment.
Puisque du mal sont le commencement,
C'est bien raison qu'ilz en souffrent la peine.
Endurez donc, pauvres yeulx, doulcement
Le doeil yssu de la joye incertaine.

If my grief can give you pleasure while another gives you greater joy, no longer fear to make me unhappy and leave the torment to my eyes. Since they are the root of grief, it is just that they suffer the pain. Then sweetly endure, poor eyes, the sorrow that issues from uncertain joy.

Pierre Regnault adopted the pseudonym "Sandrin" from a character in a fifteenth-century musical farce. It has been suggested that as a youth, the composer played in these farces. His chansons were first published in 1538, and in the following year, his name appeared as dean of St.-Florent-de-Roye in Picardy. By 1543, Sandrin belonged to the Chapel Royal of Francis I, and at the king's death in 1547, he was listed as *composeur*. Sometime in the 1550s, Sandrin left the court for Italy, where he died after 1561.

Among his chansons, "Sy mon travail vous peult donner plaisir" and "Doulce memoire en plaisir consommée" became favorites throughout the sixteenth century. "Sy mon travail vous peult donner plaisir" is a simple homophonic work in the conventional mold of the Parisian chanson. One of the traits common to many Parisian chansons at this time is the use of one specific rhythmic pattern for every musical phrase of the work. In "Sy mon travail vous peult donner plaisir," it is a three-note upbeat usually on the same pitch followed by a descending or ascending scale in eighth notes. The scale usually functions as a flourish on the fourth syllable of the poetic line or at the end. By repeating this rhythmic formula in every phrase of this chanson, Sandrin unifies his miniature work.

This particular poem was also employed by two other composers, Crecquillon and Manchicourt. The latter used Sandrin's superius as an invertible canon between the two upper voices of his five-part version. In addition, this Sandrin chanson inspired a musical response—the next chanson, "Le dueil issu de la joye incertaine."

SOURCES: RISM: 1538^{11} f. 7v (re-ed: 1540^{9} f. 7v), 1549^{17} f. 13v, 1551^{4-5} f. 24, 1554^{25} f. 9, 1560^{6} p. 35 (re-ed: 1562^{3} p. 18, 1570^{8} p. 18, 1573^{4} f. 18, 1576^{2a} f. 18, 1589^{5} f. 18, 1592^{8} f. 18, 1597^{9} f. 18, 1601^{4} f. 18, 1605^{5} f. 18, 1608^{11} f. 18, 1609^{12} f. 18, 1613^{7} f. 18, 1617^{6-6a} f. 18, 1632^{5} f. 18, 1633^{2} f. 18, 1640^{6} f. 18, 1644^{3} f. 18); *Premier livre du Recueil* . . . (Du Chemin: 1567), f. 2v; Brown: 1547_{9}, 1549_{8}, $154?_{5}$, 1552_{11}, 1563_{12}, 1568_{6}, 1568_{7}, 1570_{3}, 1571_{6}, 1582_{5}; Dublin, Trinity College MS D.3.30/I, p. 246; York, Yorkminster Lib., M.91 (S), f. 112v; The Hague, Koninklijke Bibl. MS 74.H.7, f. 43v; Regensburg, Proske Bibl. MS A.R. 940/41, no. 139, Basel, Univ. Bibl. MS F.X. 22–24, no. 26.

MODERN EDITIONS: Albert Seay, ed., *Pierre Sandrin, Collected Works, Corpus Mensurabilis Musicae* 47 (1968), p. 10.

EMENDATIONS: The whole note used in all voices for the second ending at bar 10 does not appear in 1538^{11} but is in 1549^{17} and all subsequent editions.

TEXT: Anonymous, *La fleur de poesie françoyse* . . . (Lotrian: 1543)

11. Le dueil issu de la joye incertaine

P. de Villiers

Le dueil issu de la joye incertaine
Permect aux yeulx seullement le pleurer.
De l'endurer dont vous aures la peine
Avec celluy qui vous peult demeurer.
O quel malheur a voulu procurer
Qu'ayez perdu au change pour choisir.
C'est double dueil qu'il vous fault endurer,
Si mon travail vous peult donner plaisir.

Uncertain joy brings sorrow, and that leads only to weeping. Enduring this, then, you add more grief to that you already suffer. Oh what misfortune has contrived to bring this about that you should lose simply by choosing. It is double sorrow you must endure, if my grief gives you pleasure.

This Villiers work presents us with an example of the *responce* chanson. Occasionally composers would offer their own replies to the more popular chansons of the day. The *responce*, often set as a dialogue with the initial chanson, contained textual and/or musical references to the original. Sometimes the chanson pairs shared the same opening melodic motive, but the main connection between the two chansons occurred in the text, as in the case of Villiers's "Le dueil issu de la joye incertaine," which begins with the last line and ends with the first line of "Si mon travail vous peult donner plaisir."

Jacques Moderne first printed the Villiers chanson in 1538. Moderne was the first publisher to break the Parisian monopoly on music printing in France by establishing his own press in Lyons, the cosmopolitan trading center and gateway to Italy. He entered into lively competition with Attaingnant, often borrowing chansons from the Parisian's publications to fill his own collections. He also introduced the works of composers not represented in the Parisian repertory of Attaingnant, such as P. de Villiers.

The origins of Villiers, like those of so many sixteenth-century composers, are unknown. His prominence in Moderne's anthologies, however, strongly suggests that he was a native of Lyons. He set many texts of Lyonnais poets like Maurice Scève, and even employed the Lyonnais dialect in one of his chansons. "Le dueil issu de la joye incertaine" became his most popular work; it continued to accompany Sandrin's "Si mon travail vous peult donner plaisir" well into the seventeenth century. Curiously, this celebrated response has never before been issued in modern edition.

SOURCES: RISM: 1538[17] f. 6. With the exception of RISM 1538[11] (which contains a setting of "Le dueil issu . . . " by Maillart) and 1554[25], all the sources cited for Sandrin's "Si mon travail . . . " are the same for the above chanson. In RISM 1560[6] to 1644[3], this chanson is listed as the response to "Si mon travail . . . " and is attributed to Sandrin. Brown: 1547[9], 1552[11], 1563[12], 1568[6], 1570[3], 1571[6], 1582[5].

12. Jouyssance vous donneray

[Clément Marot]

Antoine Gardane

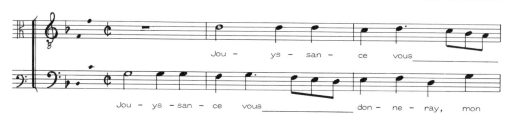

Jou - ys - san - ce vous

Jou - ys - san - ce vous don - ne - ray, mon

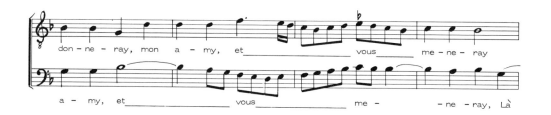

don - ne - ray, mon a - my, et vous me - ne - ray

a - my, et vous me - ne - ray, Là

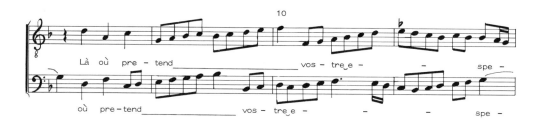

Là où pre - tend vos - tre e - spe -

où pre - tend vos - tre e - spe -

ran - ce; Vi - van - te ne vous lays -

- ran - ce; Vi - van - te ne vous lays -

- se - ray, En - cores, quant mor - te se - ray, quant mor -

- se - ray, En - cores, quant mor - te, mor -

Jouyssance vous donneray,
Mon amy, et vous meneray
La où pretend vostre esperance;
Vivante ne vous laysseray,
Encores, quant morte seray,
L'esprit en aura souvenance.

Pleasure will I give you my beloved, and I will lead you where your hope aspires. While I live, I will never leave you, and even in death, my spirit will always remember.

During the second quarter of the sixteenth century, music printers responded to the needs of amateur instrumentalists by publishing arrangements of their favorite works.

In addition to the transcriptions for keyboard and intabulations for fretted instruments, arrangements of chansons for fewer than four voices were issued in an attempt to accommodate the ever-widening circle of amateur players and singers.

Most of these two- and three-part arrangements were the work of house-editors employed by music printers, or of the publishers themselves who dabbled in musical composition. One of these "composer-publishers" was Antoine Gardane, or, to use the better-known Italian form of his name, Antonio Gardano. A French musician, as he called himself, Gardano set up his press in Venice, where he published madrigals, motets, and *canzoni francese* from 1538 until his death in 1572.

In his two-part version of *Jouyssance vous donneray*, Gardano elaborates the bass part of Claudin's chanson (no. 1 above). The highly patterned figuration strongly suggests that this arrangement was intended primarily for instruments rather than for voices.

SOURCES: RISM: 1539^{21} p. 23 (re-ed: 1544^{14}, 1552^{16}, 1564^{13}, 1586^{6}), 1540^{7} # 90, 1545^{6} # 24; Munich, Bayer. Staatsbibl. Mus. MS 260, no. 100.

MODERN EDITION: B. Bellingham and E. Evans, eds., *Sixteenth Century Bicinia, Recent Researches in Music of the Renaissance*, 15–17 (Madison, Wis.: 1974), p. 179.

TEXT: See Claudin's "Joyssance vous donneray" (no. 1 above).

13. Tru, tru, trut avant il fault boire

Jean Richafort

Tru, tru, trut avant il fault boire

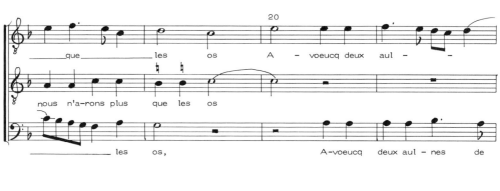

Tru, tru, trut avant il fault boire!
Car apres que serons mors,
Nous n'arons plus que les os
Avoeucq deux aulnes de toille.
Tru, tru, trut avant il fault boire!

Fie, fie, a fig's end, let's drink up! For after we are dead, we'll have nothing but our bones in two ells of cloth. Fie, fie, a fig's end, let's drink up!

While the Parisians moved toward a simple homorhythmic texture in their chansons, composers from the Low Countries continued to explore the contrapuntal idiom of their predecessors. One of the forms they inherited was the three-part arrangement of popular tunes, a type of chanson that enjoyed a great vogue in the early years of the sixteenth century, particularly at the court of Louis XII.

Composers such as Antoine de Févin, Jean Mouton, and the Flemish master, Josquin des Pres, were fond of using melodies, often associated with the French secular theater, as the basis of their polyphonic chansons. They composed these chansons by first placing the borrowed tune in the tenor part and then adding outer voices in imitation. In such arrangements, each phrase begins with the outer voices followed by the tune in the tenor; at the end of the phrase, all three voices cadence together.

The texts of these popular chansons, like their simple tunes, contrast greatly with those of their courtly predecessors. Free from the fixed forms and complicated rhyme schemes of the rondeau and ballade, these popular poems are written in a direct colloquial language. The texts deal with a wide variety of subjects mostly of the middle and lower classes. Love still remains the dominant theme, but the idealized, spiritual variety of the courtly world gives way to an earthy, frank one. Love is either satirized or portrayed in naïve, pastoral surroundings. The cuckolded husband, lecherous monk, and shepherd and shepherdess all make their appearance in these colorful vignettes. Songs of a political or historical nature also occur in the popular lyric, as does the familiar drinking song. The formal structures of these poems conform to their commonplace themes in that syllable counts between lines often differ and rhyme schemes are either loosely constructed or simply do not exist.

By 1520, younger contemporaries, such as the Netherlander, Jean Richafort, began to compose in this three-part form. Born in Hainaut around 1480, Richafort served as choirmaster at the church in Malines when Margaret of Austria, Regent of the Netherlands, resided there. He could have acquired his skill at writing these borrowed tune chansons from Josquin, of whom he might have been a pupil, or perhaps while he was in Rome at the Papal court of the Francophile, Leo X, where he possibly spent some time around 1513. By 1531, he returned to the service of the Hapsburg court. Residing in Bruges, he became musical director at St. Giles' Church and remained there until his death around 1547.

His drinking song, "Tru, tru, trut avant il fault boire," illustrates the three-part chanson in its later stages. The melodic lines of all three parts are concise, and the text setting remains syllabic throughout. The formal structure resembles the more modern shape of the Parisian chanson, with its repetition of the initial section at the end and compact proportions.

Sources: RISM: 1536[1] f. 13v, 1542[8] #79.

14. Au joly boys je rencontray m'amye

Clemens (non Papa) (?)

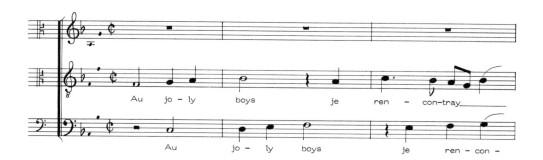

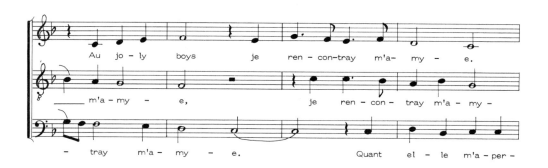

Au joly boys je rencontray m'amye

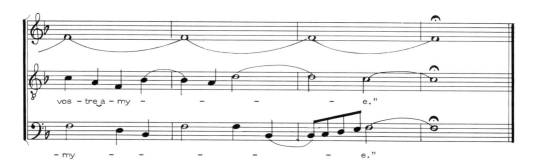

72

Au joly boys je rencontray m'amye.
Quant elle m'aperceut elle fut resjouye.
Elle m'a dit tout bas en soubriant:
　　"Baisez moy tant, tant,
　　Fringuez moy tant, tant,
　　Je seray vostre amye."

In the pretty woods I met my sweetheart, and she rejoiced to see me. Softly she whispered with a smile: "Kiss me some more, frig me some more, I will be your beloved."

Along with Nicolas Gombert, Jacob Clemens is considered one of the leading Netherlandish composers of the mid-sixteenth century. Since many of his chansons were published by Attaingnant during the 1530s, one might conjecture that he was in Paris for his years of apprenticeship. Clemens might have spent the last part of his life in the Flemish towns of Ieper and also Dixmuiden, where he was buried in 1555 or 1556.

This three-part chanson is an arrangement of a popular melody. "Au joly boys je rencontray m'amye" with its catchy tune and risqué text became a favorite in the French capital. The tune was published in all sorts of arrangements for solo keyboard, lute, and guitar, and it was even transformed into a dance, the stately pavane. The above version first appeared anonymously in an Attaingnant publication of 1529. Only in a posthumous print issued by the Flemish printer, Pierre Phalèse, two years after the death of Clemens is it ascribed to the composer. The attribution to Clemens is thus dubious.

Unlike the Richafort chanson we have encountered, "Au joly boys je rencontray m'amye" contains three voices that share equally in the presentation of the borrowed tune. The texture of this chanson remains imitative throughout. Both the quick rhythmic pace and constant imitation brilliantly express the carefree mood of the poem, especially at the end of the refrain where the continuous repetition of the same short motive by all three voices conveys the maiden's flirtatious whispers.

Sources: RISM: 1529[4] f. 17, 1560[7] f. 7 (re-ed: 1569[10] f. 7).

Modern Edition: K. Ph. Bernet Kempers, ed., *Jacobus Clemens non Papa, Collected Works, Corpus Mensurabilis Musicae* 4 (1962), X, p. 1.

15. Baises moy tant, tant

Adrian Willaert

> *"Baises moy tant, tant,*
> *Fringues moy tant, tant,*
> *Mon amy je vous prie;*
> *Baises moy tant, tant,*
> *Fringues moy tant, tant,*
> *Si seray vostre amie."*

Au joli bois je rencontrai m'amye.
Quand m'aperceut elle fut resjouye.
Elle m'a dit tout bas en souriant:
> *"Baises moy tant, tant, . . .*

"Kiss me some more, frig me some more, I beg you my dearest; kiss me some more, frig me some more, I will be your beloved."

In the pretty woods I met my sweetheart, and she rejoiced to see me. Softly she whispered with a smile: "Kiss me some more . . . "

Adrian Willaert (c. 1490–1562), a Netherlander by birth, spent the major part of his life in Italy. As *maestro di cappella* at St. Mark's Cathedral, he introduced to Italian musicians the Franco-Netherlandish style of composition and established Venice as a leading musical center.

Like Clemens, Willaert based his three-part chanson on the popular Parisian tune, "Au joli bois je rencontrai m'amie." This chanson, in fact, is one of three different settings of the tune by Willaert. The middle section, with its three-voice texture, melody in the tenor, and imitative entries, typifies the French chanson of the 1520s. But in contrast to the Clemens version, the shifts in meter, chordal texture, and quick dotted rhythms of the refrains in the Willaert setting betray a more modern outlook.

Willaert and Clemens were not the only composers intrigued by this tune; Gombert borrowed the melody for a six-voice setting, and Pierre Certon, in turn, replaced its racy text with a much tamer contrafactum, "J'ay le rebours de ce que je souhaite." This chanson can be performed in a number of ways: by three voices, three instruments, two instruments for the outer parts with solo voice on the tenor, or any sort of instrumental doublings of vocal parts.

SOURCES: RISM: 1536[1] f. 10v, 1562[9] p. 27, 1578[16] f. 14v; *Cincquiesme livre de chansons composé à troys parties par M. Adrian Willart* . . . (Le Roy & Ballard: 1560) f. 8.

16. Joissance vous donnerai

[Clément Marot]

Adrian Willaert

Joissance vous donnerai

Joissance vous donnerai,
Mon amis, et vous meneray
Là où pretend vostre esperance;
Vivante ne vous laisseray,
Encore, quant morte serai,
L'esprit en aura souvenance.

*Pleasure will I give you my beloved, and I will lead you where your hope aspires. While I live,
I will never leave you, and even in death, my spirit will always remember.*

By the middle of the sixteenth century, Netherlandish composers began to incorporate
melodies from Parisian chansons as borrowed material for their own polyphonic works.
Just as the popular tunes of earlier decades of the century influenced serious composers,
so too did the freely invented melodies of Claudin and other Parisian composers affect
the Netherlanders. In these so-called "paraphrase chansons," the composer borrows
one of the vocal lines (often the superius) from a Parisian chanson and presents it in either its original or an elaborated form in a number of voices of his own chanson. The
paraphrase chanson differs from the earlier three-part arrangement in that all the
voices share in the development of the borrowed tune.

Willaert chose the tenor part of Claudin's "Joyssance vous donneray" (see no. 1
above) for his five-voice setting. The paraphrased tune appears in a relatively unelab-
orated form, but Willaert obscures the Claudin tenor by moving it from part to part.
The opening motive, for example, begins in the superius, shifts at bar 4 to the tenor
part and then, at bar 6, repeats in the alto. Unlike its model, the Willaert version is
through-composed. The overlapping of phrases and constant imitation are also stylistic
traits commonly found in the mid-century Netherlandish chanson. It must be pointed
out that the above chanson was copied from the earliest extant print, *Selectissimae
necnon familiarissimae cantiones* of 1540 published by the German, Melchior Kriesstein.
In this source, the chanson has a key signature of one flat. In all subsequent sixteenth-
century editions, however, Willaert's piece contains no flat in the key signature and is
transposed down a fourth.

SOURCES: RISM: 1540[7] #44, 1545[14] f. 2, 1572[2] f. 1, 1588[31], p. 8; *Livre de Meslange
. . .* (Le Roy & Ballard: 1560); Brown: 1566[3], 1572[1], 1573[1], 1584[2], 1599[11]; Paris, Bibl. nat.
MS Rés Vm[a] 851, p. 489.

MODERN EDITIONS: Charles Jacobs, ed., *1572 Mellange de Chansons* (University Park, Pa.:
1982), p. 29.

EMENDATIONS: *Text:* bars 6–7, tenor originally "mon amis et vous meneray"; bars 16–
20, superius originally "mon amis et vous meneray"; bars 17–23, quintus originally "mon amis
et vous meneray"; bars 22–29, superius originally "là où pretend vostre esperance"; bars 23–28,
contratenor originally "là où pretend vostre esperance"; bars 23–27, tenor originally "là où pretend vostre esperance"; bars 23–24, bassus originally "là où pretend vostre esperance"; bars
31–34, tenor originally "encore quant morte serai"; bars 30–33, bassus originally "encore
quant morte serai"; bars 38–41, quintus originally "l'esprit en aura souvenance"; bars 41–42,
contratenor originally began with "encore quant morte serai."

Music: bar 24, beat 3, superius half note instead of 2 quarters; bar 33, beat 3, tenor half note
instead of 2 quarters; bar 38, beat 4, tenor originally an e'.

TEXT: See Claudin's setting (no. 1 above).

17. Jouissance vous donneray

[Clément Marot]

Nicolas Gombert

Jouissance vous donneray

88

91

93

Jouissance vous donneray

Jouissance vous donneray,
Mon amy, et vous menneray
La où pretent vostre esperance;
Vivante ne vous laisseray,
Encor, quant morte je seray,
Si vous auray en souvenance.

Pleasure will I give you my beloved, and I will lead you where your hope aspires. While I live, I will never leave you, and even in death, I will always remember you.

Nicolas Gombert was one of the great contrapuntalists of the sixteenth century. The exact date and place of Gombert's birth remain unknown, but by 1526 he was serving in the domestic chapel of Charles V as a singer. Some three years later, when the composer accompanied the Emperor from Spain through Northern Italy, Austria, and Germany, he had been elevated to the post of master of the children. Gombert was appointed a canon at Tournai in 1534 and apparently spent the last years of his life there.

Gombert's fame rests primarily upon his sacred works, including ten masses and more than one hundred and sixty motets. He also composed over seventy chansons. "Jouissance vous donneray" serves as a fine example, not only of Gombert's secular style, but also of the paraphrase chanson, for it, too, is based on the Claudin chanson included in this anthology (see no. 1 above).

The tenor part from Claudin's work dominates the Gombert setting, but in contrast to Willaert's setting (see no. 16 above) which only employs the tenor line, Gombert's version adopts other voices from the Claudin model as well. The texture of Gombert's chanson also sounds entirely different from its homorhythmic model, for Gombert fragments Claudin's melodic lines into short motives to be expanded and developed, so that his work increases to almost double the length of Claudin's. In his paraphrase, Gombert makes the phrases overlap, blurring the cadential points and creating a continuous flow of elaborately worked-out counterpoints. Moreover, the use of six voices with its additional contratenor and bass parts darkens the timbre. Note, too, the use of cross-relations at bars 26, 44, 55, the last of which is commonly called the "English cadence" because of the English predilection for this harmonic clash. In general, the dense texture, low tessitura, and close points of imitation make this chanson a lush, hauntingly beautiful work.

SOURCES: London, British Library, Royal Appendix MSS 49–54, f. 15.

MODERN EDITIONS: Joseph Schmidt-Görg, ed., *Nicolas Gombert, Collected Works, Corpus Mensurabilis Musicae* 6 (1975), XI, p. 220.

TEXT: See Claudin's setting (no. 1 above).

18. Il me suffit de tous mes maulx

Cornelius Canis

Il me suffit de tous mes maulx

Il me suffit de tous mes maulx

Il me suffit de tous mes maulx

Il me suffit de tous mes maulx,
Puis qu'ilz m'ont livré à la mort.
J'ay enduré peine et travaulx,
Tant de douleur et desconfort.
    Que voulez que je face
    Pour estre en vostre grace?
De douleur mon coeur si est mort
    S'il ne voit vostre face.

I have had enough of all my ills, since they have almost been my death. I have endured pain and hardship, so much suffering and grief. What shall I do to win your favor? My heart languishes if I do not see your face.

Aside from paraphrase techniques, canon provided a prime means of organization in the mid-century polyphonic song. The use of canon in the French chanson is almost as old as the genre itself. The great fourteenth-century composer Guillaume de Machaut wrote a celebrated chanson incorporating a retrograde canon and appropriately entitled it: "Ma fin est mon commencement, et mon commencement ma fin." A century later, Guillaume Dufay occasionally had recourse to canonic devices in chansons such as "Entre vous, gentils amoureux," and "Puisque vous estez campieur."

When the fixed forms, which had dominated the chanson for two centuries, began to lose favor at the turn of the sixteenth century, composers retained the time-honored canonic method as a means of organization. Many chansons by Josquin des Pres, for example, contain sustained canons. "Baises moy" exists in both double and triple-canonic versions. The two lower voices of the four-part "Plus nulz regretz" form a canon at changing time and pitch intervals, and "Faulte d'argent" incorporates a canon based on the popular tune of that name.

Mid-century composers, particularly those of Netherlandish origin, continued to employ canonic techniques in their secular compositions. Following the example of earlier composers, this later generation also maintained the practice of incorporating preexistent material into its compositions, not only the old popular tunes that had been used by their predecessors, but also melodies borrowed from the chansons of Claudin and the Parisians. Among these Parisian tunes was Claudin's "Il me suffit de tous mes maulx." Arranged for various instruments and then transformed into a basse dance, the tune was appropriated by Cornelius Canis, Thomas Crecquillon, and Antoine Mornable, who all composed canonic chansons upon it.

The Netherlander Canis first appears in 1542 in the Netherlands chapel of Charles V at Madrid. In 1547, he succeeded Gombert as master of the children, and two years later accompanied Philip II on his entry into Ieper. He retired from the Imperial service by 1557 when he went to Courtrai. Canis died in Prague in 1561.

His six-voice version of "Il me suffit de tous mes maulx" employs Claudin's tune in a three-part canon between the tenor and two upper voices, surrounded by three freely invented voices. As in most canonic pieces, the imitative voices are not written out in any of the four original part-books; instead, a canon or rule placed above the leading part instructs the remaining canonic voices when to enter. In the Canis chanson, the motto above the tenor part: "Superius in diapason secundus contratenor in diapenthe," tells the two upper voices to begin an octave and then a fifth above the tenor respectively.

SOURCES: RISM: 1546[12] f. 1v (re-ed: 1546[13] f. 1v).

EMENDATION: bar 34, beat 3, contratenor 1 originally an a.

TEXT: Anonymous, *S'ensuyvent plusieurs belles chansons nouvelles* . . . (Lotrian: 1535); modern edition: Brian Jeffery, ed., *Chanson Verse of the Early Renaissance*, Vol. II, pp. 237–38.

19. Ung gay bergier prioit une bergiere

Thomas Crecquillon

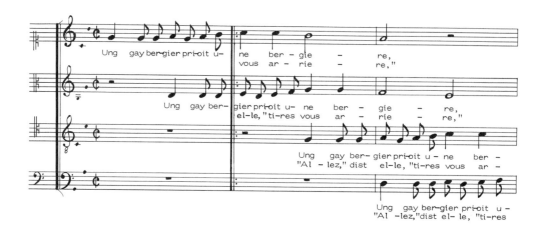

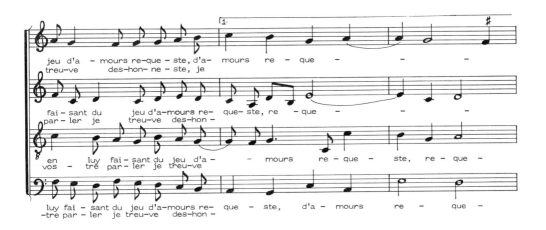

Ung gay bergier prioit une bergiere

Ung gay bergier prioit une bergiere
En luy faisant du jeu d'amours requeste.
"Allez," dist elle, "Tires vous arriere,
Vostre parler je treuve deshonneste.
Ne penses pas que feroie tel deffault;
Parquoy cessez faire telle priere,
Car tu n'a pas la lance qu'il me fault."

A shepherd begs his lady, throwing down the challenge of love. "Withdraw," she says, "I find you unworthy. Trouble me no more, nor think I shall succumb, for your weapon is not to my taste."

Like Canis, Thomas Crecquillon belonged to the *grande chapelle* of the Netherlands chapel of Charles V. His position in the chapel, however, remains unclear. From 1555, he held a canonicate at Bethune, where he probably died in 1557. Contemporaries praise Crecquillon as one of the outstanding composers of the age, and their esteem is verified by the numerous chansons by the composer printed, not only in his native country, but also in France, Germany, and Italy. The two leading Flemish publishers, Susato and Phalèse, include twice as many chansons by Crecquillon as by the nearest competitors, Gombert, Clemens, and even Lassus. Susato devoted an entire edition to Crecquillon—an honor reserved for only three other composer: Josquin, Lassus, and Manchicourt.

"Ung gay bergier prioit une bergiere" emulates the clear, precise style of the Parisian chanson. Its quick imitative counterpoint, vocal pairings, and chordal middle section in triple time, as well as its lascivious subject, remind us of many chansons by Janequin, Certon, and Passereau. It appeared in many collections of lute music as well as manuscripts intended for instrumental consort. This chanson was most influential, however, as a model for keyboard works. The Spanish composer Antonio de Cabezon wrote a *glosa* on Crecquillon's chanson, and one of Andrea Gabrieli's *canzoni francese* is also based on the Flemish work. Perhaps its suggestive text had something to do with its success in arrangements for lute, keyboard, and instrumental consorts. More likely though, its widespread fame can be attributed to the chanson's lively rhythmic pace and lucid texture.

SOURCES: RISM: 1543^{16} f. 16, 1550^{10} p. 26, 1560^6 p. 30 (re-ed: 1562^3 p. 38, 1570^8 p. 38, 1573^4 f. 38, 1576^{2a} f. 7, 1589^5 f. 7, 1592^8 f. 7, 1597^9 f. 6v, 1601^4 f. 6v, 1605^5 f. 6v, 1608^{11} f. 6v, 1609^{12} f. 6v, 1613^7 f. 6v, 1617^{6-6a} f. 6v, 1632^5 f. 6v, 1633^2 f. 6v, 1640^6 f. 6v, 1644^3 f. 6v); Brown: 1545_3, 1547_7, 1547_9, 1552_{11}, 1553_1, 1557_2, 1558_5, 1563_{12}, 1568_1, 1568_7, 1571_6, 1573_3, 1574_5, 1577_6, 1577_7, 1578_3, 1582_1 [attrib. to Janequin], 1584_2, [1586]$_2$, 1591_2, 1591_3, 1592_{10}, 1599_7; London, British Lib. Additional MS 31390, f. 103; Cambridge, Fitzwilliam Museum MS 52.A.30–33, f. 32v; Dublin, Trinity College MS D.3.30/I, p. 248; York, Yorkminster Lib. M.91 (S), f. 37v; Vienna, Oesterreichische Nat. Bibl. MS 18811, f. 68v; Basel, Univ. Bibl., MS F. IX. 59–62, no. 73; Basel, Univ. Bibl., MS F. IX. 50, p. 13.

MODERN EDITIONS: Franz Commer, ed., *Collectio operum musicorum batavorum saeculi XVI* (Berlin: 1858), 12, p. 28. Hugo Riemann, ed., *Handbuch der Musikgeschichte* (1901–1913), II, p. 462.

TEXT: Anonymous, *La fleur de poesie françoyse . . .* (Lotrian: 1543). This poem occurs in the literary source as a ten-line stanza (dizain) that elaborates upon the sexual pun of the last line.

20. Le bergier et la bergiere

Jean Lecocq

Le bergier et la bergiere

la ber-gie-re sont à l'om-bre d'ung buis   —   son.

à l'om — bre d'ung buis   —   son. Ils   sont   si

— son.   Ils   sont   si   pres

et   la   ber-gie-re sont   à   l'om — bre d'ung buis — son.   Ils   sont

— re   sont à l'om-bre d'ung   buis   —   —   son. Ils   sont   si

Ils   sont   si   pres   l'ung de   l'au — tre,

pres,   ils   sont   si   pres   l'ung   de   l'au — tre,

ils   sont   si   pres   l'ung de l'au   —   tre,   ils

si   pres   l'ung de   l'au — tre,   ils   sont

pres   l'ung de   l'au — tre,

ils sont si pres l'ung de l'au-tre Qu'à grant pei - ne les

ils sont si pres l'ung de l'au - tre Qu'à grant pei - ne

sont si pres l'ung de _____ l'au - tre Qu'à grant pei - ne les

si pres l'ung de l'au-tre Qu'à grant pei - ne les voit on, les

ils sont si pres l'ung de ____ l'au - tre Qu'à grant pei-ne

voit _____ on. La da - me a dict à son mi -

les ____ voit on. La da - me a dict, la da - me a dict à

voit ___ on. La da - me a dict, à son mi -

voit _____ on. La da - me a dict à

les ____ voit on. La da - me a dict à son mi - gnon:

Le bergier et la bergiere

-tons, mon com-pai-gnon, Pour dieu gar- dons la ____ lai - - ne, Le - ne!"

nos mou-tons, mon com-pai-gnon, Pour dieu gar-dons la lai - ne, lai - ne, le

-tons, mon com-pai-gnon, Pour dieu gar- dons la lai-ne, le loup em-

nos mou-tons, mon com-pai-gnon, Pour dieu saul-vez la lai - ne, lai - ne!"

-tons, mon com-pai-gnon, Pour dieu saul- vez la lai - - ne, Le - ne, le

loup em-por- te nos mou-tons mon com-pai-gnon, pour dieu saul-vez la lai - ne!"

-por- te nos mou-tons, mon com-pai- gnon, pour dieu saul-vons la lai - ne!"

loup em-por- te nos mou-tons, mon com-pai-gnon, pour dieu saul-vons la lai - ne.!"

115

Le bergier et la bergiere
Sont à l'ombre d'ung buisson.
Ils sont si pres l'ung de l'autre
Qu'à grant peine les voit on.
La dame a dict à son mignon:
"Reprenons nostre allaine,
Le loup emporte nos moutons, mon compaignon,
Pour dieu saulvez la laine!"

The shepherd and shepherdess are now lying in the shade of a tree. They are so close to each other that you can scarcely distinguish them. The lady says to her sweetheart, "Quick let's catch our breath; the wolf is carrying our sheep away, my dearest, for God's sake you must save the wool!"

Another chanson on a pastoral theme, "Le bergier et la bergiere" can be thought of as a companion to Crecquillon's "Ung gay bergier prioit une bergiere." The use of quick, repeated notes and wide intervals makes this chanson particularly conducive to performance by an instrumental consort. "Le bergier et la bergiere," in fact, appears in English instrumental manuscripts alongside the indigenous *In Nomine*, and the fantasia.

   The identity of Jean Lecocq, or Joannes Gallus as he is called in some sources, remains uncertain. It seems fairly clear that he is not the same as Maistre Ihan of Ferrara. In addition to twenty-two extant chansons, he wrote nine Latin motets. Most of his works were published in the Low Countries. The text of this chanson was first set in a three-part version by the composer Renez, and was reset by Gombert, Certon, and Derick Gerarde, a Netherlander who lived in England.

SOURCES: RISM: [1543]¹⁵ f. 14; London, British Library, Additional MS 31390 f. 103, Additional MS 22597, f. 33, Additional MS 32377 f. 56.

TEXT: Anonymous, *S'ensuyvent plusieurs belles Chansons* . . . (Lotrian: 1535); modern edition: Brian Jeffery, ed., *Chanson Verse of the Early Sixteenth Century*, Vol. II, p. 299.

21. Si par souffrir l'on peult vaincre Fortune

Jean Courtois

Si par souffrir l'on peult vaincre Fortune,
Je croy en plus le prix me demourer;
Car nuict et jour je ne fais que penser
A ma douleur et soubdaine infortune.

If by suffering one can conquer fortune, then I believe that the victory is mine; for night and day I do nothing but think of my sorrow and sudden ill-fate.

While many Netherlandish composers were connected with the Imperial court or traveled to Italy in hopes of gaining appointments, a few musicians became attached to the musical establishments of great northern cathedrals. The Cathedral of Notre Dame at Cambrai was one of the most illustrious choir-cathedrals of Northern Europe. In the fifteenth century, numerous musicians, including the great composer Guillaume Dufay, received their musical training there.

Cambrai's reputation continued to flourish when Jean Courtois became choirmaster in 1540. Of his eleven chansons published from 1529 to 1539, "Si par souffrir l'on peult vaincre Fortune" is a particularly beautiful example of the courtly chanson. Its somber, low vocal ranges and haunting melodic line reflect the melancholy vein of the poem. The chanson appeared in a variety of sixteenth-century anthologies, and achieved some popularity as an instrumental pavane which the printer, Tylman Susato of Antwerp, published in his *Danserye . . .* of 1551. This chanson can be performed equally well by voices or instrumental consort, or even by a solo voice on the top part with lute or viol accompaniment.

SOURCES: RISM: 1534^{14} f. 3, 1540^7 #55, 1544^{12} f. 6; Brown: 1546_9, 1551_8, 1562_3; Cambrai, Bibl. de la Ville, MS 125–128, f. 123v; London, British Lib. Royal Appendix MS 41–44, f. 8v, f. 11v; Danzig, Stadtbibl., MS 4003, Bk. I, no. 56; Munich, Bayer. Staatsbibl. Mus. MS 1501, p. 16.

MODERN EDITION: Robert van Maldeghem, ed., *Tresor musical, Musique profane* (Brussels: 1880), 16, p. 34 (appears with substitute text: "Or tout plaisir").

TEXT: Anonymous, appears as the third stanza of "O doulce amour . . . " in *S'ensuyvent plusieurs belles Chansons . . .* (Lotrian: 1535); modern edition: Brian Jeffery, ed., *Chanson Verse of the Early Renaissance*, II, p. 293.

22. Je ne sçay que c'est qu'il me fault

[Mellin de Saint-Gelais]

Antoine Mornable

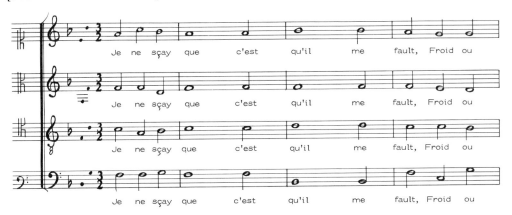

Je ne sçay que c'est qu'il me fault, Froid ou

chault; Je ne dors plus ny je ne veil -

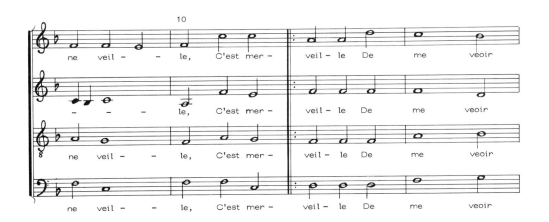

ne veil - - le, C'est mer - veil - le De me veoir

1. Je ne sçay que c'est qu'il me fault,
   Froid ou chault;
   Je ne dors plus ny je ne veille,
   C'est merveille
   De me veoir sain et langoureux;
   Je croy que je suis amoureux.

[2. En quatre jours je ne fais pas
   Deux repas,
   Je ne voy ne beufs ne charrue;
   J'ay la rue
   Pour me promener nuict et jour
   Et fuy l'hostel et le sejour.]

[3. Aussi il m'estoit grand besoin
   D'avoir soin
   Qui aurait des danses le prix:
   J'y fus pris,
   Et m'amusay tant à la feste,
   Qu'encores m'en tourne la teste.]

4. Je ne sçay où le mal me tient,
   Mais il vient
   D'avoir dansé avec Catin.
   Son tetin
   Alloit au bransle, maudit sois je,
   S'il n'estoit aussi blanc que neige.

[5. Elle avait son beau collet mis
   De Samis,
   Son beau surcot rouge et ses manches
   Des dimanches,
   Un long cordon à petits noeuds
   Pendant sur ses souliers tous neufs.]

6. Je me vi jetter ses yeulx vers
   De travers;
   Dont je feiz des saulz plus de dix,
   Et luy dis,
   Et luy serrant le petit doy:
   "Catin, c'est pour l'amour de toy!"

122

7. Sur ce point elle me laissa
  Et cessa
De faire de moy plus de compte:
  J'en euz honte
Si grande que pour me boucher
Je feiz semblant de me moucher.

[8. Je l'ay veue une fois depuis
  A son huis,
Et une autre allant au marché;

J'ay marché
Cent pas pour luy dire deux mots.
Mais elle me tourne le dos.]

9. Si ceste contenance fiere
  Dure guere,
A dieu grange, à dieu labouraige!
  J'ay couraige
De me veoir gendarme un matin,
Ou moyne en despit de Catin.

I do not know what I want: hot or cold. I can neither sleep nor wake. It puzzles me, that I am well but languish. I think I'm in love.

[In four days I have but eaten twice. Nor ox, nor cart I see. Night and day I walk the street fleeing the hostel and my rest.]

[My greatest care has been to guess who would win the dancing prize. I was so caught up with the festivities that my head still spins.]

I do not know where the sickness possesses me, but it comes from having danced with Catin. Her breasts moved with the dance, and I'll be damned if they were not as white as snow.

[She had her beautiful collar of silk, her lovely red tunic with finest Sunday sleeves. A long ribbon with tiny knots hanging down to her brand new shoes.]

I saw her green eyes glance at me sideways, whereupon I did more than ten jumps and told her while holding her little finger: "Catin, it is for the love of you!"

At this point she left me, and ceased to pay me any attention. I was so ashamed that in order to stifle myself, I pretended to blow my nose.

[I have seen her once since then at her door, and one other time going to market. I walked a hundred steps to say two words to her, but she turned her back on me.]

If her pride continues then farewell farm and field. I have the courage to wake up one morning and become a soldier or a monk just in spite of Catin!

In the sixteenth century, the humanist movement, which had taken hold in Italy a century before, began to affect the literary circles of Paris. Proclaiming as their goal a revival of the union between poetry and music of classical times, the humanists advocated solo singing of French verses to the accompaniment of the lute in order to capture the ideal sound of the Greek lyre. Although the movement did not reach its zenith until mid-century, a court poet from the previous generation, Mellin de Saint-Gelais, accomplished this sacred union with his verses.

Along with Marot, Saint-Gelais introduced the Italian sonnet and epigram into the French language. His odes and lyric poems inspired musical settings by mid-century composers like Arcadelt and Mornable. Not only a talented poet, Saint-Gelais was apparently a skilled musician as well, for contemporaries describe him as singing his poetry at court while accompanying himself with a lute.

Saint-Gelais's strophic verses formed a perfect match with the new type of chanson becoming fashionable in Paris in the 1540s and 50s—the *voix de ville*. As "Je ne sçay que c'est qu'il me fault" illustrates, the *voix de ville* consists of a lyric poem in strophic form set to a simple melody sung with or without accompaniment. The accompaniments were either by solo instrument (i.e., the lute or guitar), or by singers in a strictly chordal style. The melodies used in these strophic songs were actually derived from dance rhythms such as the galliard, pavane, and branle. Contrary to the chansons of the previous generation, these tunes often appeared in the tenor part. The simplicity and neutrality of dance tunes offered a perfect partnership for the strophic lyric since the music obviously played a subordinate role to the words.

The composer of "Je ne sçay que c'est qu'il me fault," Antoine Mornable, had his early musical training in Paris, where he was a choirboy at the Sainte Chapelle until 1530. By 1546, he had left Paris to become choirmaster and music director at the court of Guy XVII, Count of Laval.

SOURCES: 1553[20] f. 5v.

TEXT: P. Blanchemain, ed., *Oeuvres Complètes de Melin de Sainct-Gelays* (Paris: 1873), 2, p. 231. Stanzas 2, 3, 5, and 8 do not appear in the original musical source but were taken from the complete works of Saint-Gelais.

23. Tout au rebours de mon affaire

Jacques Arcadelt

Tout au rebours de mon affaire

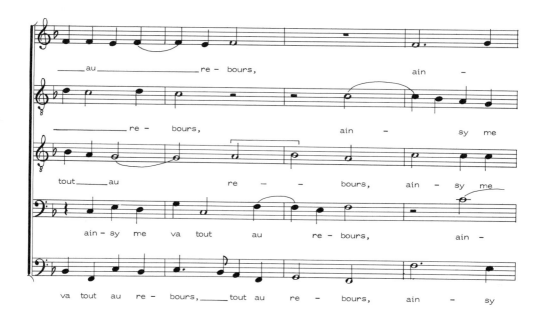

128

Tout au rebours de mon affaire
Comme il appert par mes amours.
Quand cuyde chanter, me fault taire.
Ainsy me va tout au rebours.

Everything is backwards in my life, as in my love. When I think of singing, I must hold my tongue. Everything for me goes backwards.

Although it has been claimed that Jacques Arcadelt was a Netherlander by birth, this assumption has been cast in doubt. Born around 1505, Arcadelt spent his early maturity in Italy; by the mid-thirties, he had become the leading madrigalist of Florence, one of the four important musical centers of Italy. Around 1553 Arcadelt left for Paris, where he served both Charles de Guise, the second Cardinal of Lorraine, and the king. Arcadelt's chansons soon caught the attention of the younger publishing firms of Du Chemin, and Le Roy and Ballard. The latter was quick to recognize the marketability of the composer's chansons and began to promote Arcadelt as their star composer. His name was the only one to appear in the titles of Le Roy and Ballard's anthologies (even though their collections also included works by other composers). This honor was later accorded to Orlande de Lassus.

"Tout au rebours de mon affaire" actually dates from the pre–Le Roy and Ballard era. Mentioned by Rabelais in his prologue to the fourth book of *Pantagruel* (1552), it reflects the Netherlandish predilection for canonic writing. As in Canis's chanson (see no. 18 above), the second canonic part is not written out in any of the partbooks. Instead, a canon or motto over the leading voice (in this case the superius) instructs the follower (the alto) when and how to enter. In this example, Arcadelt obscures the meaning of the motto placed above the superius part by making it a pun: *Si demandés qui je suis, commes les deux seaux d'un puis* (If anyone wants to know, I am like the two buckets of a well [one going up as the other goes down]). This motto, and the initial line of the poem as well, aptly describes the type of canon employed between the two upper voices as canon by inversion. Thus, the alto part moves in the opposite direction from the superius.

SOURCES: RISM: 1548[3] f. 6v, 1569[13] f. 16.

MODERN EDITION: Albert Seay, ed., *Jacob Arcadelt, Collected Works, Corpus Mensurabilis Musicae* 31 (1968), VIII, p. 21.

24. Qui n'a senti qu'une flamme

Jacques Arcadelt

Qui n'a sen - ti qu'u - ne flam - me, Et n'a ser - vi qu'u - ne

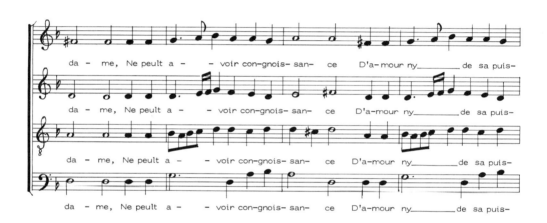

da - me, Ne peult a - - voir con-gnois- san - ce D'a-mour ny____ de sa puis-

san - ce. Et peut tou - - te_a - mour pre - mie - re Es - tre

sans _____ blas - me le - gie - re, et peut — re.

sans blas - me le - gie - re, et peut — re.

sans _____ blas - me ___ le - gie - re, et peut — re.

sans blas - me le - gie - re, et peut — re.

(Fine)

A- vec - ques trop de con- stan - ce, J'ay fait long - temps re-sis- ten - ce A mon

A- vec - ques trop de con- stan - ce, J'ay fait long - temps re-sis- ten - ce A mon

A- vec - ques trop de con- stan - ce, J'ay fait long - temps re-sis- ten - ce A mon

heur _____ et ma_for - tu - ne Pour m'ar-res - ter trop à ___ u - ne Vou-lant

heur _____ et ma for - tu - ne Pour m'ar-res - ter trop à u - ne Vou-lant

heur _____ et ma for - tu - ne Pour m'ar-res - ter trop à u - ne Vou-lant

(*D. C. al Fine*)

Qui n'a senti qu'une flamme,
Et n'a servi qu'une dame,
Ne peult avoir congnoissance
D'amour ny de sa puissance.
Et peut toute amour premiere
Estre sans blasme legiere.

(Trio):

    Avecques trop de constance,
    J'ay fait longtemps resistence
    A mon heur et ma fortune
    Pour m'arrester trop à une
    Voulant donner tesmoingnage
    De mon esprit non vollage.

Mais j'ay fait si longues preuves
Depuis, et tant d'amours neuves
Plus folles que la premiere,

Qu'une affection derniere
Sur toutes digne et honneste
A fait de mon coeur conqueste.

    Et ma flamme trop ardente
    Avecques ma vaine attente
    Par la raison amortie
    En autre s'est convertie;
    Plus constante et amoureuse,
    Et pour moy trop plus heureuse.

Que donc qu'on ne trouve estrange
De moy ce nouvel eschange,
O mes cheres damoyselles,
Subjettes à flammes telles,
Car de vous la plus acorte
Changeroit de mesme sorte.

He who has felt only one flame, and has served only one lady, cannot have known love nor its power. And every first love can blamelessly be light.

So long, with such constancy, I have fought against fate and fortune, staying too long with a single one, in order to demonstrate my faithful spirit.

But I have made more thorough proofs; since then there have been many new loves, each one madder than the last. The latest of my affections, however, worthy and upright above all others, has conquered my heart.

And my too ardent passion, my vain waiting, against all reason was transferred to another, more constant, loving, happy.

So don't think it strange then that I have changed, my dear ladies, you too have such passions, and even the most charming of you would change in the same way.

Besides Arcadelt's use of the Netherlandish contrapuntal idiom, he also acquired the homophonic *voix de ville* style prevalent at the French court. In contrast to his imitative chansons, Arcadelt's *voix de villes* were strictly chordal, strophic in form, and usually set to a particular dance rhythm.

"Qui n'a senti qu'une flamme" illustrates the most famous of these dance patterns: a triple meter dance with hemiola cadences. In the early sixteenth century, this dance pattern became fashionable in Italy, where it appeared in the instrumental saltarello and vocal frottola. In France, it was extensively used in the galliard. The rhythmic pattern never lost its popularity in dance and song throughout the sixteenth century. Even in the seventeenth century, during the formative years of Italian opera, the formula still occurred in the works of Italian composers, most notably Monteverdi.

This Arcadelt chanson consists of two sections. The second, here called a trio, is performed in alternation with the first section. The omission of one voice in the trio suggests performance by a group of soloists in contrast to a larger ensemble for the first section. The succession of different vocal combinations in one chanson was an idea eventually taken up in the seventeenth century *air de cour*.

SOURCES: RISM: 1564[11] f. 6 (re-ed: 1565[7] f. 6, 1569[16] f. 6, 1571[2] f. 6, 1575[9] f. 6, 1578[11] f. 6, 1587[2] f. 6).

MODERN EDITION: Albert Seay, ed., *Jacob Arcadelt, Collected Works, Corpus Mensurabilis Musicae* 31 (1968), IX, p. 80.

25. Las, voules vous q'une personne chante Orlande de Lassus

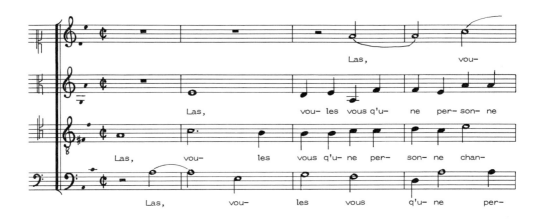

134

Las, voules vous q'une personne chante

Las, voules vous q'une personne chante
A qui le coeur ne fait que souspirer?
Laisses chanter celui qui se contente,
Et me laisses mon seul mal endurer.

My heart is sighing; yet alas, you ask for song. Let those sing who are happy, and leave me to endure my single grief.

Arcadelt's successor as leading composer in the Parisian publications of Le Roy and Ballard was the Netherlander, Orlande de Lassus. No other sixteenth-century composer achieved such widespread fame as Lassus. His works issued from all the major European publishing houses. He mastered and excelled in all musical genres, from the motet and mass to the madrigal, chanson, and German song. Through him, the chanson acquired characteristics associated with the madrigal.

Born in Mons in 1532, Lassus might have received his early musical training at the church of St. Nicholas. At the age of twelve, he entered into the service of Ferrante Gonzaga, Viceroy of Sicily. He spent most of his early years in Italy. In 1555 he went to Antwerp, and a year later he left for Munich where he served at the court of Duke Albrecht V, and then the duke's son Wilhelm, until his death in 1594.

Lassus's first published works appeared at both Antwerp and Venice in 1555 when he was only twenty-three years old. "Las voules vous q'une personne chante" was the opening chanson in the Antwerp collection. As an early work, it displays the composer's interest in the Italian madrigal with its great variety of melodic ideas, general expressiveness, and occasional use of word painting as on the word *chanter*.

Lassus's taste in French texts is as diverse as his musical compositions; it encompasses the popular verse associated with the early sixteenth-century theater, of which this chanson is an example, as well as the sophisticated sonnets of Ronsard and the Pléiade. Although "Las voules vous q'une personne chante" originated as a popular song, this setting is not based upon a pre-existing tune. Because of the expressive nature of the chanson, vocal performance is preferable.

SOURCES: RISM: 1555^{19} f. 1v (re-ed: 1555^{29} f. 1v, 1560^4 f. 1v), 1557^{10} f. 8, 1559^{12} f. 7 (re-ed: 1561^5 f. 6, 1565^6 f. 2, 1569^{15} f. 6, 1572^4 f. 2, 1575^7 f. 6, 1583^6 f. 2); *Tiers livre des chansons . . . par Orlando di Lassus* (Phalèse: 1560; re-ed: 1562, 1566, 1570, 1573); *Les Meslanges D'Orlande de Lassus* (Le Roy & Ballard: 1570; re-ed.: 1576, 1586); Brown: 1568_7, 1571_6, 1574_1, 1574_2, 1577_6; Florence, Bibl. Medicea-Laurenziana MS Ashburnham 1085, f. 41; Paris, Bibl. nat. MS Rés 255, f. 41.

MODERN EDITIONS: A. Sandberger, ed., *Orlando di Lasso, Sämtliche Werke* (Leipzig: 1900), 12, p. 3. Henry Expert, ed., *Les Maîtres musiciens de la Renaissance française, Les Meslanges d'Orlande de Lassus* (Paris: 1894), I, p. 1.

TEXT: Anonymous, *Les chansons nouvellement assemblées . . .* (1538); modern edition: Brian Jeffery, ed., *Chanson Verse of the Early Renaissance*, Vol. II, p. 345.

26. Susane un jour d'amour solicitée

[Guillaume Guéroult]

Orlande de Lassus

Susane un jour d'amour solicitée

Susane un jour d'amour solicitée

je fay re - sis - tan — ce, Vous me fe - rez mou —

je fay re - sis - tan — ce, Vous me fe - rez mou - rir en

je fay re - sis - tan - ce, Vous me fe - rez mou - rir

je fay re - sis - tan — ce, Vous me fe - rez mou —

je fay re - sis - tan - ce, Vous me fe - rez mou - rir _____ en

- rir en des — hon - neur; Mais j'ay-me mieux pe -

des — — hon - neur; Mais j'ay-me mieux, mais j'ay-me mieux pe -

en des — — hon - neur; Mais j'ay-me mieux, mais j'ay - me

- rir en des - hon - neur; Mais j'ay - me mieux

des - hon - neur; Mais j'ay - me mieux, mais j'ay-me mieux

Susane un jour d'amour solicitée
Par deux viellards convoitans sa beauté,
Fut en son coeur triste et desconfortée
Voyant l'effort fait à sa chasteté.
Elle leur dit: "Si par desloyauté
De ce cors mien vous avez jouissance
C'est fait de moy; si je fay resistance,
Vous me ferez mourir en deshonneur;
Mais j'ayme mieux perir en innocence,
Que d'offencer par peché le Seigneur."

Susanna fair, sometime of love requested
By two old men, whom her sweet looks allur'd,
Was in her heart full sad and sore molested,
Seeing the force her chastity endur'd.
To them she said: "If I, by craft procur'd,
Do yield to you my body to abuse it,
I kill my soul; and if I shall refuse it,
You will me judge to death reproachfully.
But better it is in innocence to choose it
Than by my fault t'offend my God on high."

In 1548, a four-part *voix de ville* by the Lyons composer, Didier Lupi II, appeared in print. The text Lupi selected for his chanson was a dizain entitled "Susanne un jour d'amour solicitée" by Guillaume Guéroult. Both composer and poet intended their work for Protestant devotional use as a *chanson spirituelle*, but the dramatic Apocryphal tale of Susanna and the Elders combined with Lupi's versatile melody greatly appealed to other composers. In fact, thirty-seven different versions of the text by more than

146

twenty-five composers appeared in prints spanning the century from 1556 to after 1642.

Lassus's five-part setting was by far the most famous. First published in Paris in 1560, the Lassus chanson went through over ten reprintings, appeared in a variety of instrumental arrangements, and even became the model for the works of other composers. Andrea Gabrieli, for example, used the Lassus chanson in a *canzona francese* for keyboard.

Across the channel, the Lassus chanson became well known in English translation. The above translation is, in fact, taken from Nicholas Yonge's *Musica Transalpina* of 1588, where the Lassus version appeared along with one by Alphonso Ferrabosco. The keyboard composer, Giles Farnaby, based his "Susanna fair" on the superius part of Lassus's setting, and even the great English composer, William Byrd, made two settings of his own using another English translation (see no. 27 below).

Like the majority of composers who set the Guéroult poem, Lassus employed Lupi's tenor as a cantus firmus, placing the borrowed line in the tenor where it remains (except at bar 22 when it exchanges parts with the quintus) for the entire piece. In general, Lassus followed the A A B A (A) form of his model. In spite of the strict construction of his tenor part, Lassus actually focussed the melodic interest of the chanson in the top part. The contrast between this appealing melody in the superius and the complex structure of Lassus's music, coupled with so compelling a subject, probably accounts for its attraction by both professional and amateur musicians of the sixteenth century.

SOURCES: RISM: 1567^8 f. 14 (re-ed: 1571^1 f. 14, 1575^8 f. 14, 1578^{10} f. 14, 1591^4 f. 14); *Tiers livre des chansons . . . par Orlando di Lassus* (Phalèse: 1560; re-ed: 1562, 1566, 1570, 1573); *Livre de Meslanges . . .* (Le Roy & Ballard: 1560); *Les Meslange d'Orlande de Lassus . . .* (Le Roy & Ballard: 1570; re-ed: 1576, 1586); Brown: 1563_{12}, 1566_3, 1568_7, 1571_1, 1571_6, 1572_1, 1573_1, 1573_3, 1574_1, 1575_3, 1577_6, 1578_3, 1582_1, 1582_5, 1584_2, 1584_6, 1591_2, 1592_6, 1593_7, 1599_7; London, British Lib. Additional MS 33933 f. 77v, Additional MS 36484 f. 7, Additional MS 30485 f. 51v, Additional MSS 29372-7, Egerton MS 3665 f. 199v, Egerton 995; Cambridge, Univ. Lib. MS Dd.2.11, f. 23v; Oxford, Christ Church College MSS 984-8 p. 78; Dublin, Trinity College MS D.3.30/I, pp. 100, 138; York, Yorkminster Lib. M.91 (S), f. 123v; Paris, Bibl. nat. MS Rés Vm^a 851, p. 509, Munich, Bayer. Staatsbibl. Mus. MS 1501, no. 52.

MODERN EDITION: A. Sandberger, ed., *Orlando di Lasso, Sämtliche Werke* (Leipzig: 1901), 14, p. 29.

TEXT: Guillaume Guéroult, *Premier livre de chansons spirituelles, par Guillaume Gueroult . . .* (Lyon: Beringen, 1548)

27. Susane un jour d'amour solicitée

[Guillaume Guéroult]

Cipriano de Rore

Susane un jour d'amour solicitée

150

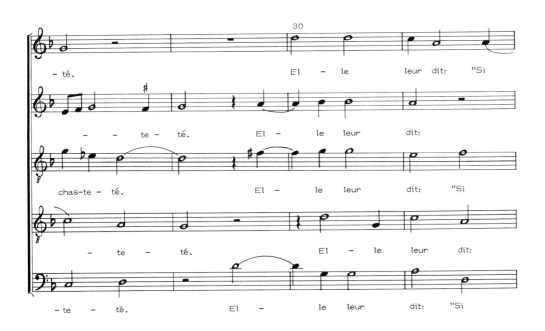

Susane un jour d'amour solicitée

- rez mou - rir en des -hon-neur; Mais j'ay -

- rir, mou - rir en des - hon - neur;

mou-rir, mou - rir en des - hon - neur; Mais

- rez mou - rir en des - hon - neur;

mou - rir, mou - rir en des - hon - neur; _____

me mieux, mais j'ay - me mieux pe - rir,

Mais j'ay - me mieux, mais j'ay - me mieux pe - rir,

j'ay - me mieux, mais j'ay - me mieux pe - rir,

Mais j'ay - me mieux pe - rir, pe - rir en in - no -

Mais j'ay - me mieux pe - rir en

Susane un jour d'amour solicitée
Par deux viellarts convoitans sa beauté,
Fut en son coeur triste et desconfortée
Voyant l'effort fait à sa chasteté.
Elle leur dit: "Si par desloyauté
De ce cors mien vous avez jouissance
C'est fait de moy; si je fay resistance,
Vous me ferez mourir en deshonneur;
Mais j'ayme mieux perir en innocence,
Que d'offenser par peché le Seigneur."

Susanna faire sometime assaulted was,
By two olde men, desiring their delight,
Whose false intent, they thought to bring to passe,
If not by tender love, by force and might.
To whome she said, "If I your sute deny,
You will me falsely accuse, and make me die,
And if I graunt to that which you request,
My chastitie shall then defloured bee,
Which is so deere to mee that I detest
My life, if it berefted bee from mee;
And rather would I dye of mine accord,
Ten thousand times, then once offend the Lord.

Cipriano de Rore, like Willaert, Arcadelt, and Lassus, was an *ultramontane*. Born in 1515 or 1516, he left his native Netherlands while still in his early twenties for Italy. He was to spend most of his life in Northern Italy, first associated in the 1540s with

Willaert in Venice, then as head of the chapel of Hercules II, Duke of Ferrara. After a brief stay (from 1558 to 1560) in his native land, Rore entered the service of the Duke of Parma. In 1563, at the death of Willaert, he was appointed chapel master at St. Mark's in Venice. This position lasted for only one year, however, for in 1564 Rore returned to Parma, where he died in 1565.

Rore's fame as a sixteenth-century composer primarily rests upon his Italian madrigals, but he also tried his hand at chanson composition. These included the inevitable setting of "Susanne un jour d'amour solicitée" which he probably composed during his sojourn in the Low Countries. Like the Lassus version, Rore's chanson is based upon the Lupi *chanson spirituelle*; it also retains Lupi's tenor as a cantus firmus. In contrast to Lassus, Rore's freer treatment of the borrowed tenor allows it to roam from the tenor parts to the superius and back again. In this through-composed work, Rore generally avoids the extreme madrigalisms associated with the French chanson at this time, perhaps because of the "sacred" nature of the text. Yet, the declamatory repetition of the words *C'est fait de moy* and the expressive climax at the end of the piece offer us a highly dramatic rendering of the popular poem. The English translation offered for this setting is taken from William Byrd's *Psalms, Sonnets and Songs of Sadness* of 1588.

SOURCES: RISM: 1570[5], 1572[2] f. 9, 1583[8] f. 11 (re-ed: 1585[12] f. 11); Tenbury, Tenbury College MS 389, f. 107.

MODERN EDITION: Charles Jacobs, ed., *1572 Mellange de Chansons* (University Park, Penn.: 1982), p. 71.

TEXT: See no. 26 above.

28. Musiciens qui chantez à plaisir

Hubert Waelrant

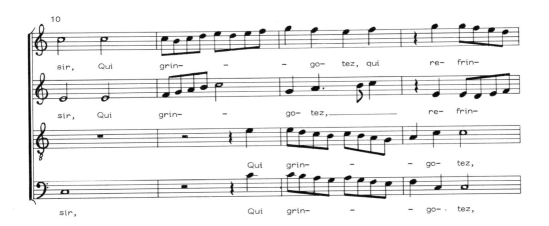

159

la li- no- te qui prend plai- sir, qui prend plai-sir en

la li- no- te qui prend plai-sir, qui prend plai-sir, qui prend plai-sir en

la li - no - - te qui prend plai- sir, qui prend plai-sir en

la li- no- te qui prend plai- sir, qui prend plai-sir en

son chant gra- - - ti- eux. Soy- ez ex- perts, soy- ez ex-

son chant gra- ti- eux. Soy- ez ex- perts, soy- ez ex-

son chant gra- - - ti- eux. Soy- ez ex-

son chant gra- ti- eux. Soy- ez ex- perts,

– perts, soy- ez ex- perts des o- reil- les et yeux Ou au- tre-

– perts, soy- ez ex- perts des o- reil- les et yeux Ou au- tre-

– perts, soy- ez ex- perts des o- reil- les et yeux

soy- ez ex- perts des o- reil- les et yeux

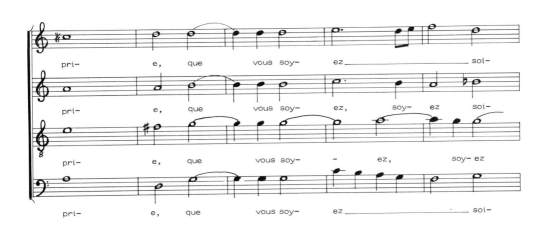

163

Musiciens qui chantez à plaisir

Musiciens qui chantez à plaisir,
Qui gringotez, refringotez la note;
Prenez un ton plus doux et à loysir
Signifiant ce que le chant denote.
Accordez vous ainsi que la linote
Qui prend plaisir en son chant gratieux.
Soyez experts des oreilles et yeux
Ou autrement il vaudroit mieux vous taire;
Et je vous prie que vous soyez soigneux
De ne chanter si vous n'avez à boire!

Musicians, you who sing at will, who improvise, divide the note; take a tone most sweet and slow signifying what the song means. Keep in tune like the linnet who takes pleasure in her graceful song. Be alert of ears and eyes or otherwise keep silent; and take good care not to sing unless you have had plenty to drink!

When Lassus returned from Italy in the 1550s, he brought with him many of the stylistic characteristics of the Italian madrigal, which began to make their way into the chanson. Netherlanders gave up their abstract, dense contrapuntal style in favor of greater delicacy and freedom in the handling of vocal lines, and a different sensitivity to the musical setting of the words. Expression became the most important facet of musical composition.

"Musiciens qui chantez à plaisir" demonstrates these madrigalian tendencies of the late sixteenth-century chanson. The florid passages on *gringotez* and *refringotez*, the sustained chordal section at *prenez un ton*, and the use of rests after *taire* all reflect a new enthusiasm for Italianate word painting. Declamatory setting, another Italian trait, occurs at such phrases as *Accordez vous* and *Et je vous prie.*

In contrast with other Northern composers at this time, Hubert Waelrant did not serve at any court, either native or foreign, but took up more commercial aspects of music during his long life (c. 1517–1595). He and the printer Jean Laet established a publishing firm in Antwerp in 1554, where Waelrant issued his own works as well as those of other composers. He was also active as a singer and theorist, and he founded a music school. Waelrant is also remembered as one of the earliest theorists to employ a solmization system based on the octave rather than the hexachord. Please note that in editing this chanson, original note values have been retained.

Sources: RISM: 1589[5] f. 13 (re-ed: 1592[8] f. 13, 1597[9] f. 13, 1601[4] f. 13, 1605[5] f. 13, 1608[11] f. 13, 1609[12] f. 13, 1613[7] f. 13, 1617[6-6a] f. 13, 1632[5] f. 13, 1633[2] f. 13, 1640[6] f. 13, 1644[3] f. 13).

Modern Edition: William Barclay Squire, ed., *Ausgewählte Madrigale* (Leipzig: [19?-]), 2, p. 94.

Emendations: bar 9, beat 1, contratenor b originally flatted.

29. Sortez regretz, et allegez mon coeur

Philippe de Monte

Sortez regretz, et allegez mon coeur,
Puisque d'aymer madame se repend;
Mais si priere humaine au ciel s'estend,
Mort ou mercy soit fin à ma douleur.

Begone regrets, and lighten my heart, for my lady repents from love; but if human prayer reaches up to heaven, then death or mercy make an end to my sorrow.

Philippe de Monte, one of the most prolific composers of the sixteenth century, was born in Mechlin in 1521. After spending his youth (1542–51) in Naples, Monte returned in 1554 to his native country. The same year he sojourned briefly in England as a member of the choir of Philip II of Spain, who had just married Queen Mary Tudor. Dissatisfied, Monte left that position in 1555 and returned to Italy. In 1568, he accepted the post of musical director at the court of the Emperor Maximilian II. Monte spent the remainder of his life in the Imperial service, first in Vienna and later under Rudolph II in Prague, where he died in 1603.

Monte's chanson, "Sortez regretz, et allegez mon coeur," reflects a much older tradition for the "regrets" chanson. Composers toward the very end of the fifteenth century were fond of employing texts containing the word *regretz* in the first line. Compère, Agricola, Pierre de la Rue, and Josquin all composed chansons with such melancholy titles as: "Tous les regretz qui les cueurs tourmentez," "Venes, regretz, venes, il en est heure," "Revenez tous, regretz, je vous convie," and the most famous regret chanson, Josquin's "Mille regretz de vous abandonner." Many of these chansons appear in the elaborate manuscripts from the collection of Margaret of Austria, the twice-widowed Regent of the Low Countries who ruled from 1507 to 1530. They reflect the somber, courtly vein evidently fashionable at the Netherlandish court during this time.

This same melancholy mood prevails in Monte's "Sortez regretz, et allegez mon coeur." The music conveys the doleful poem with its rich harmonic palette and simple melodic motive of a descending minor second.

Sources: RISM: 1567[11] f. 1 (re-ed: 1570[13] f. 1, 1573[13] f. 1, 1577[5] f. 1, 1581[2] f. 1).

Modern Edition: G. van Doorslaer, ed., *Philippe de Monte: Opera Omnia* (Düsseldorf: 1932), 20, p. 9.

30. Margot labourez les vignes bien tost

Jean de Castro

Margot labourez les vignes bien tost

172

Margot labourez les vignes bien tost,
  Vigne, vigne, vignolet,
Margot labourez les vignes bien tost.

En revenant de Loraine,
  Margot [labourez les vignes]
Rencontray trois capitaines,
  Vigne, vigne, vignolet,
  Margot labourez les vignes bien tost.

Ilz m'ont salué vilaine;
  Margot [labourez les vignes]
Je suis leurs fievres cartaines.
  Vigne, vigne, vignolet,
  Margot labourez les vignes bien tost.

Margot, till the vineyard very early, vineyard, vineyard, vineyard, hey; Margot, till the vineyard very early.

While returning from Lorraine (Margot, till the vineyard), I met three captains (Vineyard, vineyard, vineyard, hey; Margot, till the vineyard very early).

They greeted me, "Hey, peasant!" (Margot, till the vineyard). I am their quartan fever (Vineyard, vineyard, vineyard, hey; Margot, till the vineyard very early).

"Margot labourez les vignes bien tost," a song of folk origin, is best known in the polyphonic settings by both Arcadelt and Lassus. These two versions adhere to the folk idiom in their simple tunes and chordal texture. Castro's delightful three-part version, on the other hand, is neither homophonic nor folk-like in its melodic style. The use of voice-pairings, dialogues, and syncopation at the refrains marks the originality of the Netherlandish composer who, along with Lassus, was considered by the Antwerp publisher, Plantin, to be his best-selling composer. This particular chanson is best suited for a trio of women's voices. Note that original note values have been retained in the editing of this chanson.

SOURCES: RISM: 1569[10] f. 20, 1574[3] p. 23; *Livre de chansons . . . à troys parties par Jo. Castro* . . . (Le Roy & Ballard: 1575), f. 9.

31. Plus est servy et plus se plaint

Guillaume Costeley

175

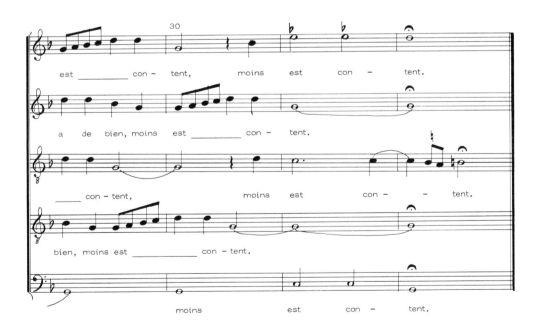

Plus est servy et plus se plaint.
Plus est nourry et plus se faint.
Plus est paré, plus se pourmeine.
Plus est aimé, plus fait de peine.
Tant plus est cru, plus souvent ment.
Plus a de bien, moins est content.

The more we have, the more we complain. The more we feed, the more we hunger. The less our need, the more our desire for gain. The more we are loved, the more we are troubled. The more we are believed, the more we lie. The better our lot, the less our contentment.

Returning to Paris in the second half of the sixteenth century, we find a confluence of chanson styles. Although the Italianate idiom undeniably became the dominant influence upon the French chanson, traditional styles continued in the works of Parisian composers. Guillaume Costeley wrote in a variety of styles.

Born around 1530 in Fontanges, Auvergne, Costeley served at the court of Henry II and his successor, Charles IX. Besides the Italianate vein, he composed homophonic *voix de villes* or light parlando counterpoint so fashionable in Paris in the 1550s. "Plus est servy et plus se plaint" exhibits the more contrapuntal idiom. Built textually on a series of antitheses, the chanson reflects the sober mood of the time. Costeley's gentle, expressive setting, in turn, highlights the sententious tone of the poem.

Sources: RISM: 1567[11] f. 15 (re-ed: 1570[13] f. 15, 1573[13] f. 15, 1577[5] f. 15, 1581[2] f. 15); *Musique de Guillaume Costeley* . . . (Le Roy & Ballard: 1570), p. 60 (re-ed: 1579 p. 60).

32. Nous voyons que les hommes

Guillaume Costeley

Nous voy-ons que les hom — mes Font tous ver - tu d'ay - mer,

Nous voy-ons que les hom — mes Font tous ver - tu d'ay -

Nous voy-ons que les hom — mes Font tous ver - tu d'ay -

Nous voy-ons que les hom — mes Font tous ver - tu d'ay -

Et sot — tes que nous som — mes Vou-lons l'a-mour bla -

-mer, Et sot — tes que nous som — mes Vou-lons l'a — mour bla -

-mer, Et sot — tes que nous som — mes Vou-lons l'a -mour bla -

-mer, Et sot — tes que nous som — mes Vou-lons l'a — mour bla -

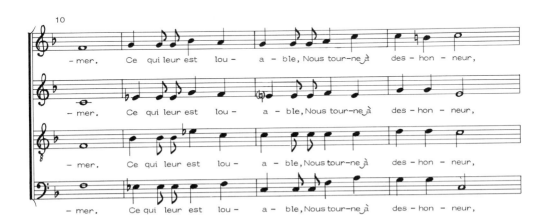

- mer. Ce qui leur est lou — a — ble, Nous tour-ne à des — hon — neur,

- mer. Ce qui leur est lou — a — ble, Nous tour-ne à des — hon — neur,

- mer. Ce qui leur est lou — a — ble, Nous tour-ne à des — hon — neur,

- mer. Ce qui leur est lou — a — ble, Nous tour-ne à des — hon — neur,

Nous voyons que les hommes
Font tous vertu d'aymer,
Et sottes que nous sommes
Voulons l'amour blamer.
Ce qui leur est louable,
Nous tourne à deshonneur.
O faute inexcusable,
O dure loy d'honneur.

Nature plus qu'eux sage
Nous a en un corps mis
Plus propre à cest usage
Et nous est moins permis.
O peu de congnoissance
De leur trop grand vouloir
Et de leur impuissance
Et de notre pouvoir.

O malheureuse envie
Des hommes rigoreux
Qui privent notre vie
Des plaisirs amoureux.
Si des le premier age
Ce sexe audacieux

Par injure et outrage,
Voulut forcer les cieux.

Et si fut si moleste
Jadis au Dieu des dieux
Osant son feu celeste
Porter en ces bas lieux,
Ce n'est point de merveille
S'il nous a aussi fait
Presque injure pareille
Sans luy avoir meffait.

Ayans par sa malice
Introduit finement
Qu'aymer ne seroit vice
Qu'aux femmes seullement,
Si leur outrecuidance
Sceurent punir les dieux
Nous avons esperance
Qu'ilz nous vengeront d'eux.

Et sera la vengeance:
Les uns mourans d'avoir
Eu trop de jouissance,
Les autres de le voir.

We see that men make love a virtue, and fools that we are, we blame love for the fault. What for them is praiseworthy, for us is dishonorable. Oh what injustice! Honor is a stern law.

Nature, more wise than men, has given us a body more fitted for love, but we do not have the freedom to use it. Oh how little do we understand men's great will, their impotence, and our power.

Oh unfortunate envy of harsh men who deprive our lives of love's pleasures. Thus in the earliest times this bold sex by insult and outrage wished to storm the heavens.

And it was such an affront to the god of gods; daring to carry his heavenly fire into these low places, it is, therefore, no wonder that he has insulted us even if we wronged him not.

Since through his malice he introduced the idea that to love would only be a vice to women alone, if the gods knew how to punish their presumptuousness, then we would hope to have our revenge.

And the vengeance will be: some would die of too much pleasure, and the others would die of envy.

In addition to neutral, light contrapuntal chansons, Costeley also composed *voix de villes*. "Nous voyons que les hommes" is a well-known strophic poem that Arcadelt set for three voices. This spirited anonymous poem is written in the feminine voice. In contrast with other chanson texts, "Nous voyons que les hommes" deals not with unrequited love, but with the unjust inequality of the sexes—a true feminist tract of the sixteenth century.

Like most *voix de villes*, Costeley's setting is a simple strophic song with chordal accompaniment. The duple meter suggests the dance rhythm of the pavane, the slow processional dance prevalent in the early sixteenth century.

SOURCES: *Musique de Guillaume Costeley . . .* (Le Roy & Ballard: 1570), p. 4 (re-ed: 1579 p. 4).

TEXT: Poem appears anonymously with a different tune in Jehan Chardavoine's *Le Recueil des plus belles et excellentes chansons en forme de voix de ville* (Paris: 1576).

33. Povre coeur entourné de tant de passions
Claude Le Jeune

- tré de tant de maux que je sens

de tant de maux que je sens, que je sens en mes vei –

de maux que je sens en mes vei – nes,

Ou – tré de tant de maux que je sens en mes vei –

de tant de maux que je sens en mes vei – nes,

en mes vei – nes, Quel – le fin au – rons-nous, quel –

– nes, Quel – le fin, quel – le fin au – rons – nous un jour à

Quel – le fin au – rons-nous, quel – le fin au – rons –

– nes, Quel – le fin au – rons – nous

Quel – le fin au – rons – nous

185

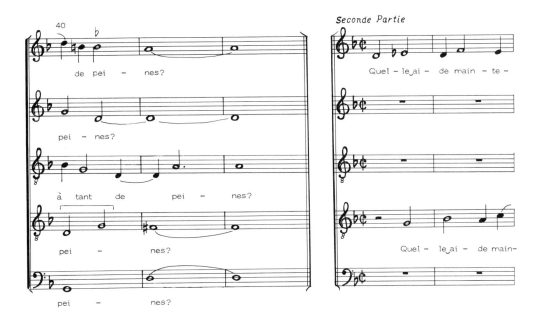

Povre coeur entourné de tant de passions

189

Povre coeur entourné de tant de passions

- tre sa - lut vou - lons nous, et quel au - tre sa - lut

Et quel au - tre sa - lut vou - lons nous, vou -

- lut, et quel au - tre sa - lut vou - lons nous

au - tre sa - lut vou-lons nous, et quel au - tre sa - lut

- lut, et quel au - tre sa - lut vou - lons

vou - lons nous d'a - van - ta - ge? Nos - tre ai - de,

- lons nous d'a - van - ta - ge? Nos - tre ai -

d'a - van - ta - ge, d'a-van - ta - ge? Nos - tre ai-de,

vou - lons nous d'a - van - ta - ge? Nos-tre ai- de,

nous d'a - van - ta - ge? Nos - tre ai - de, nos -

Povre coeur entourné de tant de passions

Povre coeur entourné de tant de passions,
De tant de nouveautez, de tant de fictions;
Outré de tant de maux que je sens en mes veines,
Quelle fin aurons-nous un jour à tant de peines?

Quelle aide maintenant, quel espoir de guerir?
Quel bon Dieu qui nous vint à ce coup secourir?
Quel port en ceste mer, quels feux en cest'orage?
Et quel autre salut voulons nous d'avantage?
Nostre aide, nostre espoir, nostre Dieu, nostre port,
Noz feux, nostre salut sont ores en la mort.

Poor heart beset by so many passions, by so many changes, so many lies. Consumed by so many evils I feel in my veins, will there ever come a day to end my woes?

What help now? What hope of cure? What good God will come to succor me? What port in this sea? What light in this storm? And what other help do we desire more? Our help, our hope, our God, our port, our light, our salvation are near in death.

While a few French composers remained loyal to the traditional chanson, others experimented with a variety of styles taken from both native and foreign sources. Claude Le Jeune was the most versatile composer in Paris during the latter part of the sixteenth century. Born in the Flemish town of Valenciennes around 1530, Le Jeune, unlike his great contemporary Lassus, who went southeast to Munich, moved to Paris in the early sixties, where he became the major musical figure in the French capital during the reigns of Charles IX, Henry III, and Henry IV. Best known for his masterpieces in the restricted style of the *musique mesurée* air, Le Jeune cultivated a variety of French forms. The paraphrase chanson based on pre-existing material, the *chanson spi-*

rituelle with its devotional texts, the obscene *chanson grivoise*, the courtly love song, and the Italianate chanson were all a part of Le Jeune's style.

One of these secular styles, the *chanson spirituelle*, grew up with the Huguenot movement in France. This para-religious form was intended for devotional use by Protestants at home. As a Huguenot himself, Le Jeune composed some forty works in this genre. Of them, "Povre coeur entourné de tant de passions" is unusual in its use of chromaticism.

The development of chromaticism in sixteenth-century secular music occurred most strikingly in the Italian madrigal. Nicolò Vicentino in the 1550s attempted to apply ancient Greek diatonic, chromatic, and enharmonic tetrachords to his own polyphonic compositions. Other madrigalists like Marenzio, Rore, and particularly Carlo Gesualdo, made novel use of chromaticism in conjunction with the emotional expression of the text. The chromaticism found in Le Jeune's *chanson spirituelle* seems to follow the tetrachord experiments of Vicentino. Although not applied in a systematic way, both chromaticism and the chromatic tetrachord are employed in "Povre coeur entourné de tant de passions." Chromatic ascending lines that span the interval of a fourth occur, for example, at *De tant de nouveautez* in the superius (bars 12–14), answered in the bass part at *de tant de fictions* (bars 17–19).

Furthermore, the chromatic tetrachord—a minor third followed by two semitones—can be traced in strict and altered forms throughout the chanson, for example, in the alto (bars 7–8), superius (bars 18–19), and the first tenor (bars 45–46). At the very end of the chanson, the chromatic tetrachord permeates the texture in continuous strettos not only in its normal ascending and descending forms (alto at bar 86, superius at bars 86–87, bass at bars 91–92, and superius at bars 94–96), but in retrograde versions as well (superius at bars 88–90, second tenor at bars 91–92, and bars 92–94).

Le Jeune employs chromaticism in this *chanson spirituelle* to heighten the dramatic aspects of the text as a whole. The extreme word painting that Gesualdo creates through chromaticism has no place in Le Jeune's work. The musical setting of the individual word remains neutral; thus, the chanson is reserved in its expression of the text. This chanson was copied from the *Meslanges de la Musique de Clau. Le Jeune*, which contains several differences from the earlier Le Roy and Ballard print, *Vingtdeuxieme Livre de chansons à quatre et cinq parties, d'Orlande de Lassus et autres* of 1583.

SOURCES: RISM: 1583[7] f. 11 (re-ed: 1585[11] f. 11); *Meslanges de la Musique de Clau. Le Jeune* . . . (Le Roy & Ballard: 1586), f. 27v (re-ed: 1587 f. 27v).

EMENDATIONS: bar 71: quintus, second beat is g in original.

34. Je suis un demi-Dieu quand assis vis à vis

[Pierre de Ronsard]

Anthoine de Bertrand

Je suis un demi-Dieu quand assis vis à vis

198

Je suis un demi-Dieu quand assis vis à vis

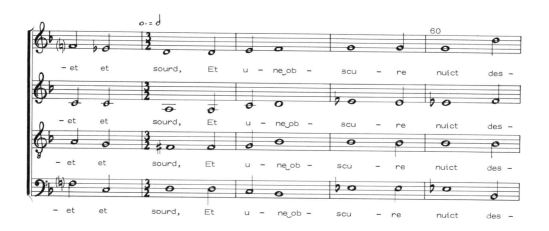

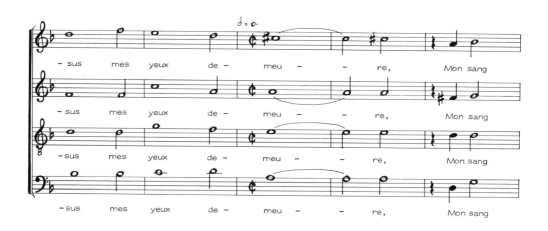

Je suis un demi-Dieu quand assis vis à vis
    De toy, mon cher soucy j'escoute les devis,
    Devis entrerompus d'un gratieux sourire,
Souris qui me detient le coeur emprisonné,
    Car en voyant tes yeux je me pasme estonné,
    Et de mes pauvres flancs un seul mot je ne tire.

Ma langue s'engourdist, un petit feu me court.
    Honteux dessous la peau, je suis muet et sourd,
    Et une obscure nuict dessus mes yeux demeure,
Mon sang devient glacé, l'esprit fuit de mon corps,
    Mon coeur tramble de crainte et peu s'en faut allors
    Qu'à tes piedz estendu, sans ame je ne meure.

I feel like a demigod when I am seated near you, my dear marigold. I hear your words, sweet words interrupted by your radiant smile, a smile which captivates my heart. When I see your eyes, I faint with amazement and become dumbfounded.

My tongue gets stuck in my throat; a small fire runs through me. So ashamed beneath my skin, I remain unable to speak or hear, and in the dark of night, my eyes can no longer see, my blood becomes ice, my spirit flees from my body, my heart trembles in fear, and I am very close to dying without a soul beneath your feet.

Pierre de Ronsard (1524–85), considered by many to be the greatest French poet of the sixteenth century, was born in Vendômois. In his youth, he traveled as a page, first to the dauphin and later to the dauphin's sister, Marguerite, who briefly before her early death became Queen of Scotland. A severe illness, which left Ronsard partially deaf, put an end to a diplomatic career at the age of sixteen. Ronsard then turned to scholarship, and along with his friends, Joachim du Bellay and Jean-Antoine de Baïf, founded a literary society which they named the Pléiade, after the seven Greek poets who likened themselves to the stars. As humanists, the Pléiade sought to establish a new French poetry based upon the ancient forms of Greece and Rome, notably the odes of Pindar and Horace. By the early part of 1550, Ronsard published his first volume of odes. In 1552, a group of sonnets entitled *Les Amours de P. de Ronsard, Vendo-*

mois appeared in print. Drawing heavily upon Petrarchan themes and conceits, *Les Amours* relates Ronsard's unrequited love for a woman named Cassandre. The popularity of this cycle induced Ronsard to issue a new edition in 1553, and in the following years, two other collections, dedicated to another woman, Marie, were also published.

"Je suis un demi-Dieu quand assis vis à vis" appeared in the *Nouvelle continuations des Amours* of 1556. This particular poem is unusual for Ronsard's *Les Amours* in that it is not a sonnet but a paraphrase of an ode by the Greek lyric poet, Sappho. The original ode appeared with a Latin translation at the end of the *L'Anacréon* of H. Estienne in 1556, and another humanist, Belleau, published his own French version at the end of his translation of the Odes of Anacreon.

From the middle of the century, Ronsard's verses were preferred by such chanson composers as Janequin, Lassus, and Costeley. Philippe de Monte and Anthoine de Bertrand, among others, devoted entire publications to his sonnets. Bertrand, in fact, set some sixty poems from the *Amours* publications.

Born in the 1540s in Auvergne, Anthoine de Bertrand spent most of his life in Toulouse, where he was associated with the humanist circle, *Academie des Jeux Floraux*. This literary group, in fact, honored Ronsard as *Poete françois par excellence*.

Bertrand, like many of his French contemporaries, was attracted to the experiments in chromaticism that were taking place in Italy. Some of his four-part chansons make use of the chromatic and enharmonic modes which Vicentino described in his theoretical writings. But above all, Bertrand excelled in the comprehension and depiction of the word in music. Thus, he avoided rhythmic and contrapuntal complexity, concentrated upon the illumination of textual details, and wrote in a clear, refined, homophonic idiom.

In "Je suis un demi-Dieu quand assis vis à vis," we see how Bertrand delicately elucidates the text in every line. The emphatic chordal entries of the voices at the very beginning portray the exaltation of the lover. The typical madrigalian gesture of quick ascending scales at *l'esprit fuit* express flight, and the trilling effect on *tramble* suggests the quivering of the heart. Bertrand even employs the madrigalian device of "eye music." In the original partbooks, the triple meter section is set in black notation to convey the darkness of *une obscure nuict*. This use of word painting is thus a visual one that the composer addressed to the performers alone. Please note that the original note values have been retained in the editing of this chanson.

SOURCES: *Second livre des Amours de P. de Ronsard . . . par Anthoine de Bertrand* (Le Roy & Ballard: 1578), f. 6v (re-ed: 1587 f. 6v).

MODERN EDITION: Henry Expert, ed., *Monuments de la Musique française au temps de la Renaissance* (Paris: 1927), 6, p. 20.

TEXT: Pierre de Ronsard, *Nouvelle Continuation des Amours* (1556); modern edition: P. Ronsard, *Oeuvres complètes*, ed. P. Laumonier (Paris: 1959), Vol. 7, p. 313.

35. Paisible demaine

Orlande de Lassus

Paisible demaine

Paisible demaine,
Amoureux verger,
Repos sans danger,
Justice certaine,
Science haultaine,
C'est Paris entier.

Peaceable kingdom, beloved bower, haven from danger, domaine of justice, land of lofty science. Paris, you are all these things.

We conclude this collection of chansons where we began it—in Paris. Although Lassus's music was issued by practically all the major publishing houses of Europe, Paris became the primary center for his chansons. In 1564, Le Roy and Ballard devoted an entire publication to the works of the great composer. Seven years later, after numerous editions of his chansons had been printed, Lassus finally visited the French capital, where he was warmly received by the French court. In 1574, Charles IX offered Lassus a handsome salary as chamber musician to the French court, but the king died before the year was out, and Lassus remained at his post in Munich. Charles's successor, Henry III, maintained friendly relations with the composer, granting him special privileges for the publication of his works.

"Paisible demaine," which appeared in 1571, the year of Lassus's trip to Paris, expresses the affection the composer held for the important center of learning and culture. This lofty setting represents the culmination of the chanson. Although Lassus, in contrast to his French contemporaries, made little use of chromaticism in his chansons, the harmonic richness, sensitivity to detail, and the great wealth of melodic invention characterize the classical ideal of the French chanson in its concluding stages. It is appropriate, then, that we end with a work by the great Netherlandish master praising the city where the sixteenth-century chanson was created.

SOURCES: *Livre de chansons nouvelles à cinc parties d'Orlande de Lassus* (Le Roy & Ballard: 1571), f. 10 (re-ed: 1576 f. 10, 1581 f. 10, 1599 f. 10); *Livre cincquiesme de chansons . . . d'Or-lande de Lassus* (Phalèse: 1571).

MODERN EDITION: A. Sandberger, ed., *Orlando di Lasso, Sämtliche Werke* (Leipzig: 1903), 16, p. 1.

List of Early Printed Sources

1528³   *Chansons nouvelles en musique a quatre parties.* Paris, P. Attaingnant, 1528.

[1528]⁵   *Trente et deux chansons musicales a quatre parties.* Paris, P. Attaingnant.

[1528]⁸   *Trente et sept chansons musicales a quatre parties.* Paris, P. Attaingnant.

1529⁴   *Quarante et deux chansons musicales a troys parties.* Paris, P. Attaingnant, 1529.

1529₃   *Tres breve et familiere introduction pour entendre & apprendre par soy mesmes a jouer toutes chansons reduictes en la tabulature du Lutz.* Paris, P. Attaingnant, 1529.

1531²   *Trente et sept chansons musicales a quatre parties.* Paris, P. Attaingnant, 1532.

1531₃   *Vingt et six chansons musicales reduictes en la tabulature.* Paris, P. Attaingnant, 1531.

1533₂   *Chansons musicales a quatre parties desquelles les plus convenables a la fleuste.* Paris, P. Attaingnant, 1533.

1534¹⁴   *Trente et une chansons musicales a quatre parties.* Paris, P. Attaingnant, 1534.

1536¹   *La Courone et fleur des chansons a troys.* Venice, A. Antico, 1536.

1536²   *Premier livre contenant XXXI. chansons musicales esleues de plusieurs livres.* Paris, P. Attaingnant, 1536.

1536³   *Second livre contenant XXXI. chansons musicales esleues de plusieurs livres.* Paris, P. Attaingnant, 1536.

1536⁴   *Livre premier contenant XXXIX. chansons a quatre parties.* Paris, P. Attaingnant, 1536.

1536⁶   *Tiers livre contenant XXI chansons musicales a quatre parties composez par Jennequin et Passereau.* Paris, P. Attaingnant, 1536.

1537³   *Second livre de chansons esleues contenant XXX.* Paris, P. Attaingnant, 1537.

1538¹⁰   *Premier livre contenant XXV chansons nouvelles a quatre parties.* Paris, P. Attaingnant and H. Jullet, 1538.

1538¹¹   *Second livre contenant XXVII chansons nouvelles a quatre parties.* Paris, P. Attaingnant and H. Jullet, 1538.

1538¹³   *Quart livre contenant XXVII chansons nouvelles a quatre parties.* Paris, P. Attaingnant and H. Jullet, 1538.

1538¹⁴   *Cinquiesme livre contenant XXVIII chansons nouvelles a quatre parties.* Paris, P. Attaingnant and H. Jullet, 1538.

1538¹⁷   *Le Parangon des chansons. Tiers livre contenant XXVI chansons nouvelles.* Lyon, J. Moderne, 1538.

1539¹⁵   *Sixiesme livre contenant XXVII chansons nouvelles a quatre parties.* Paris, P. Attaingnant, 1539.

1539¹⁶   *Sixiesme livre contenant XXVII chansons nouvelles a quatre parties.* Paris, P. Attaingnant and H. Jullet, 1539.

1539[21]   *Canzoni francese a due voci di Ant. Gardane et di altri autori.* Venice, A. Gardane, 1539.

1540[7]   *Selectissimae necnon familiarissimae cantiones ultra centum vario idiomate vocum.* Augsburg, M. Kriesstein, 1540.

1540[9]   *Second livre contenant XXVII chansons nouvelles a quatre parties.* Paris, P. Attaingnant and H. Jullet, 1540.

1540[11]   *Quart livre contenant XXVIII chansons nouvelles a quatre parties.* Paris, P. Attaingnant and H. Jullet, 1540.

1540[12]   *Cincquiesme livre contenant XXV chansons nouvelles a quatre parties.* Paris, P. Attaingnant and H. Jullet, 1540.

1540[16]   *Le Parangon des chansons. Sixiesme livre contenant XXV chansons nouvelles.* Lyon, J. Moderne, 1540.

1540[17]   *Le Parangon des chansons. Septiesme livre contenant XXVII chansons nouvelles.* Lyon, J. Moderne, 1540.

1541   *Onziesme livre contenant xxviii chansons nouvelles a quatre parties.* Paris, P. Attaingnant, 1541.

1542[8]   *Tricinia.* Wittenberg, G. Rhau, 1542.

1542[14]   *Unziesme livre contenant XXVIII chansons nouvelles a quatre parties.* Paris, P. Attaingnant, 1542.

1542[15]   *Unziesme livre contenant XXVIII chansons nouvelles a quatre parties.* Paris, P. Attaingnant and H. Jullet, 1542.

[1543][15]   *Vingt et six chansons musicales & nouvelles a cincq parties.* Antwerp, T. Susato.

1543[16]   *Premier livre des chansons a quatre parties auquel sont contenues trente et une nouvelles chansons.* Antwerp, T. Susato, 1543.

1544[7]   *Quinziesme livre contenant XXX chansons nouvelles a quatre parties.* Paris, P. Attaingnant, 1544.

1544[8]   *Quinziesme livre contenant XXX chansons nouvelles a quatre parties.* Paris, P. Attaingnant and H. Jullet, 1544.

1544[12]   *Le quatriesme livre des chansons a quatre parties auquel sont contenues trente et quatre chansons nouvelles.* Antwerp, T. Susato, 1544.

1544[14]   *Canzoni francese a due voci d'Antonio Gardane insieme alcuni de altri autori, libro primo.* Venice, A. Gardane, 1544.

1545[6]   *Bicinia gallica, latina, germanica. . . . Tomus primus.* Wittenberg, G. Rhau, 1545.

1545[14]   *Le sixiesme livre contenant trente et une chansons nouvelles a cincq et a six parties.* Antwerp, T. Susato, 1545.

1545[3]   *Des chansons reduictz en Tabulature de Lut a deux, trois, et quatre parties.* Louvain, P. Phalèse, 1545.

1546[11]   *Premier livre contenant XXV chansons nouvelles a quatre parties.* Paris, P. Attaingnant, 1546.

1546[12]   *Dixneufiesme livre contenant XXII chansons nouvelles a quatre parties.* Paris, P. Attaingnant, 1546.

1546[13]   *Dixneufiesme livre contenant XXII chansons nouvelles a quatre parties.* Paris, P. Attaingnant, 1546.

1546[9]   *Musica und Tabulatur, auff die Instrument der kleinen und grossen Geygen, auch Lauten . . . durch Hansen Gerle.* Nuremberg, Formschneider, 1546.

1546[18]   *Des chansons reduictz en Tabulature de luc a trois et quatre parties.* Louvain, P. Phalèse, 1546.

1547[12] *Vingtcinqiesme livre contenant XXVIII chansons nouvelles a quatre parties.* Paris, P. Attaingnant, 1547.

1547[7] *Des chansons Reduictz en Tabulature de Lut a deux, trois, et quatre parties.* Louvain, P. Phalèse, 1547.

1547[9] *Des Chansons & Motetz Reduictz en Tabulature de luc a quatre, cinque et six parties, livre troixiesme.* Louvain, P. Phalèse, 1547.

1548[3] *Vingt sixiesme livre contenant XXVII chansons nouvelles a quatre parties.* Paris, P. Attaingnant, 1548.

1549[17] *Premier livre des chansons esleues en nombre XXX.* Paris, P. Attaingnant, 1549.

1549[18] *Second livre contenant XXIX. chansons.* Paris, P. Attaingnant, 1549.

1549[28] *Second livre du Recueil, contenant XXVII chansons antiques a quatre parties.* Paris, N. du Chemin, 1549.

1549[8] *Carminum quae chely vel testitudine canuntur, Liber primus.* Louvain, P. Phalèse, 1549.

154?[5] *Tabulature de Lutz en diverses sortes.* Lyon, J. Moderne.

1550[6] *Tiers livre contenant XXVIII. chansons.* Paris, P. Attaingnant, 1550.

1550[8] *Tiers livre du Recueil, contenant XXIX chansons antiques, a quatre parties.* Paris, N. du Chemin, 1550.

1550[10] *Sixiesme livre, contenant XXV. chansons nouvelles à quatre parties.* Paris, N. du Chemin, 1550.

1551[4] *Premier livre du recueil contenant XXX. chansons anciennes, a quatre parties.* Paris, N. du Chemin, 1551.

1551[5] *Premier livre du recueil, contenant XXVIII. chansons anciennes, a quatre parties.* Paris, N. du Chemin, 1551.

1551[6] *Second livre du recueil, contenant XXVI. chansons anciennes, a quatre parties.* Paris, N. du Chemin, 1551.

1551[8] *Het derde musyck boexhen begrepen int ghet al van onser neder duytscher spraken.* Antwerp, T. Susato, 1551.

1552[16] *Di Antonio Gardano il primo libro de canzoni francese a due voci.* Venice, A. Gardano, 1552.

1552[11] *Hortus musarum in quo tanquam flosculi quidam selectissimorum carminum.* Louvain, P. Phalèse, 1552.

1553[20] *Premier livre contenant XXVI chansons nouvelles en musique a quatre parties.* Paris, P. Attaingnant, 1553.

1553[1] *Intabulatura valentini bacfarc transilvani coronensis.* Lyons, J. Moderne, 1553.

1554[25] *Premier recueil de chansons, composées a quatre parties.* Paris, A. Le Roy and R. Ballard, 1554.

1554[6] *Second livre de tabulature de leut, contenant plusieurs Chansons, Motetz & Fantasies.* Paris, M. Fezandat, 1554.

1555[19] *Le quatoirsiesme livre a quatre parties . . . par Rolando di Lassus.* Antwerp, T. Susato, 1555.

1555[29] *D'Orlando di Lassus il primo libro dovesi contengono madrigali, vilanesche, canzoni francesi et motetti a quattro voci.* Antwerp, T. Susato, 1555.

1557[10] *Second livre de chansons nouvellement mises en musique, à quatre parties.* Paris, N. du Chemin, 1557.

1557[2] *Libro de cifra nueva para tecla, harpa, y vihuela.* Alcala, J. de Brocar, 1557.

1558[5] *Tabulatur buch auff die Lauten.* Heidelberg, J. Kholen, 1558.

1559[12]   *Douziesme livre de chansons nouvellement composées en musique a trois, quatre, et cinq parties.* Paris, A. Le Roy and R. Ballard, 1559.

1560[4]   *Le quatoirsiesme livre a quatre parties . . . par Rolando di Lassus.* Antwerp, T. Susato, 1560.

1560[6]   *Septiesme livre des chansons a quatre parties convenables tant aux instrumentz.* Louvain, P. Phalèse, 1560.

1560[7]   *Premier livre du recueil des fleurs produictes de la divine musicque a trois parties.* Louvain, P. Phalèse, 1560.

1560[8]   *Di Clement Janequin il secondo libro de canzon francese a quatro voci.* Venice, A. Gardano, 1560.

1560[3]   *Premier livre de tablature de luth de M. Jean Paule Paladin.* Lyon, S. Gorlier, 1560.

1560   *Cincquiesme livre de chansons composé à troys parties par M. Adrian Willart.* Paris, A. Le Roy and R. Ballard, 1560.

1560   *Livre de Meslanges, contenant six vingtz chansons . . . composées à cinq, six, sept, & huit parties.* Paris, A. Le Roy and R. Ballard, 1560.

1560   *Tiers livre des chansons . . . par Orlando di Lassus.* Louvain, P. Phalèse, 1560.

1561[5]   *Douziesme livre de chansons nouvellement composé en musique à quatre, & cinq parties, par Orlande de Lassus.* Paris, A. Le Roy and R. Ballard, 1561.

1561   *Second livre du Recueil des recueilz de chansons à quatre parties.* Paris, N. du Chemin, 1561.

1561   *Tiers livre du Recueil des recueilz de chansons à quatre parties.* Paris, N. du Chemin, 1561.

1562[3]   *Septiesme livre de chansons a quatre parties.* Louvain, P. Phalèse, 1562.

1562[9]   *Il terzo libro delle Muse a tre voci. Di Canzon francese di Adrian Willaert.* Venice, G. Scotto, 1562.

1562[3]   *Lautten Buch, von mancherley schönen und lieblichen stucken, mit zweyen Lautten zusamen zu schlagen.* Strasbourg, C. Müller, 1562.

1562[10]   *Tiers livre de tabelature de luth contenant plusieurs chansons. Par Maistre Albert de Rippe Mantouan.* Paris, A. Le Roy and R. Ballard, 1562.

1562   *Tiers livre des chansons . . . par Orlando di Lassus.* Louvain, P. Phalèse, 1562.

1563[12]   *Theatrum musicum in quo selectissima optimorum quorumlibet autorum.* Louvain, P. Phalèse, 1563.

1564[11]   *Quinsieme livre de chansons à quatre cinq & six parties.* Paris, A. Le Roy and R. Ballard, 1564.

1564[13]   *Di Antonio Gardano il primo libro de canzoni francese a due voci.* Venice, A. Gardano, 1564.

1564[1]   *Premier livre de tabelature de luth . . . par Vallentin bacsarc.* Paris, A. Le Roy and R. Ballard, 1564.

1565[6]   *Douzieme livre de chansons a quatre & à cinq parties par Orlande de Lassus.* Paris, A. Le Roy and R. Ballard, 1565.

1565[7]   *Quinsieme livre de chansons à quatre cinq & six parties de plusieurs autheurs.* Paris, A. Le Roy and R. Ballard, 1556 [sic].

1566[3]   *Il secondo libro intabolatura di liuto di Melchior Neysidler Alemano.* Venice, A. Gardano, 1566.

1566   *Tiers livre des chansons . . . par Orlando di Lassus.* Louvain, P. Phalèse, 1566.

1567[8]   *Quatorsieme livre de chansons à quatre & cinq parties, d'Orlande de lassus.* Paris, A. Le Roy and R. Ballard, 1567.

1567[11] *Dixneufieme livre de chansons nouvellement composé à quatre, & cinq parties.* Paris, A. Le Roy and R. Ballard, 1567.

1567 *Premier livre du Recueil des recueilz de chansons à quatre parties.* Paris, N. du Chemin, 1567.

1568[1] *Libro Primo d'intabulatura da leuto, di M. Antonio di Becchi Parmegiano.* Venice, G. Scotto, 1568.

1568[6] *Nova Longeque elegantissima cithara ludenda carmina . . . per Sebastianum Vreed-man.* Louvain, P. Phalèse, 1568.

1568[7] *Luculentum theatrum musicum.* Louvain, P. Phalèse, 1568.

1569[10] *Recueil des fleurs produictes de la divine musicque a trois parties . . . Second livre.* Louvain, P. Ph lèse, 1569.

1569[13] *Sisieme livre de chansons à quatre & cinq parties, de I. Arcadet, & autres.* Paris, A. Le Roy and R. Ballard, 1569.

1569[15] *Dousieme livre de chansons à quatre & cinq parties, d'Orlande de Lassus & autres autheurs.* Paris, A. Le Roy and R. Ballard, 1569.

1569[16] *Quinzieme livre de chansons à quatre & cinq parties, d'Orlande de Lassus & autres autheurs.* Paris, A. Le Roy and R. Ballard, 1569.

1570[5] *Premier livre des chansons a quatre et cincq parties, composées par Orlando di Lassus, Cyprian de Rore,* Louvain, P. Phalèse, 1570.

1570[8] *Septiesme livre des chansons a quatre parties.* Louvain, P. Phalèse, 1570.

1570[13] *Dixneufieme livre de chansons à quatre & cinq parties, d'Orlande de Lassus, & autres.* Paris, A. Le Roy and R. Ballard, 1570.

1570[3] *Hortulus cytharae, in duos distinctus libros.* Louvain, P. Phalèse, Antwerp, J. Bellère, 1570.

1570 *Les Meslanges D'Orlande de Lassus.* Paris, A. Le Roy and R. Ballard, 1570.

1570 *Musique de Guillaume Costeley.* Paris, A. Le Roy and R. Ballard, 1570.

1570 *Tiers livre des chansons . . . par Orlando di Lassus.* Louvain, P. Phalèse, 1570.

1571[1] *Quatorsieme livre de chansons, à quatre, & cinq parties, d'Orlande de Lassus, & autres.* Paris, A. Le Roy and R. Ballard, 1571.

1571[2] *Quinzieme livre de chansons, à quatre, cinq & six parties, d'Orlande de Lassus, & autres.* Paris, A. Le Roy and R. Ballard, 1571.

1571[1] *Orgel oder Instrument Tabulatur. Ein nützlichs Büchlein, in welchem notwendige erklerung der Orgel oder Instrument Tabulatur, . . . Durch Eliam Nicolaum, sonst Amerbach genandt.* Leipzig, Ammerbach, 1571.

1571[6] *Theatrum musicum.* Louvain, P. Phalèse and J. Bellère, 1571.

1571 *Livre cincquiesme de chansons . . . d'Orlande de Lassus.* Louvain, P. Phalèse, 1571.

1571 *Livre de chansons nouvelles a cinc parties d'Orlande de Lassus.* Paris, A. Le Roy and R. Ballard, 1571.

1572[2] *Mellange de chansons tant des vieux que des modernes, a cinq, six, sept, et huict parties.* Paris, A. Le Roy & R. Ballard, 1572.

1572[4] *Dousieme livre de chansons à quatre & cinq parties, d'Orlande de Lassus & autres.* Paris, A. Le Roy and R. Ballard, 1572.

1572[1] *Das Erste Büch Newerlessner Fleissiger ettlicher viel Schöner Lautenstück.* Strasbourg, B. Jobin, 1572.

1573[4] *Livre septiesme des chansons a quatre parties.* Louvain, P. Phalèse, 1573.

1573[13] *Dixneufieme livre de chansons à quatre & cinq parties, d'Orlande de Lassus, & autres.* Paris, A. Le Roy and R. Ballard, 1573.

1573_1 *Tabulatura continens praestantissimas et selectissimas quasque cantiones . . . à Melchiore Neusydler.* Frankfurt, J. Eichorn, 1573.

1573_3 *Tabulatura continens insignes et selectissimas quasque cantiones, . . . per Matthaeum Waisselium.* Frankfurt, J. Eichorn, 1573.

1573   *Tiers livre des chansons . . . par Orlando di Lassus.* Louvain, P. Phalèse, 1573.

1574^3 *La Fleur des chansons a trois parties, contenant un recueil. . . . de Iean Castro, Severin Cornet, Noë Faignient & autres excellens aucteurs.* Louvain, P. Phalèse, Antwerp, J. Bellère, 1574.

1574_1 *Novae, elegantissimae, Gallicae, item et italicae cantilenae . . . per M. Sixtum Kaergel.* Strasbourg, B. Jobin, 1574.

1574_2 *A briefe and plaine Instruction to set all Musicke of eight divers tunes in Tableture for the Lute.* London, J. Rowbothome, 1574.

1574_5 *Teutsch Lautenbuch Darinnenn Kunstliche Muteten, liebliche Italianische, Frantzösische . . . durch Melchior Newsidler.* Strasbourg, B. Jobin, 1574.

1574_7 *Thesaurus Musicus continens selectissima Alberti Ripae, Valentini Bacfarci.* Louvain, P. Phalèse & J. Bellère, 1574.

1575^7 *Dousieme livre de chansons à quatre & cinq parties, d'Orlande de Lassus et autres.* Paris, A. Le Roy and R. Ballard, 1575.

1575^8 *Quatorzieme livre de chansons à quatre, & cinq parties d'Orlande de Lassus et autres.* Paris, A. Le Roy and R. Ballard, 1575.

1575^9 *Quinzieme livre de chansons à quatre, cinq, & six parties d'Orlande de Lassus et autres.* Paris, A. Le Roy and R. Ba lard, 1575.

1575_3 *Toppel Cythar. Nova eaque artificiosa et valde commoda ratio ludendae cytharae . . . Durch Sixtum Kärgel Lautenisten, und Johan Dominico Lais.* Strasbourg, B. Jobin, 1575.

1575   *Livre de chansons . . . à troys parties par Jo. Castro.* Paris, A. Le Roy and R. Ballard, 1575.

1576^{2a} *Livre septieme des chanssons a quatre parties.* Louvain, P. Phalèse, Antwerp, J. Bellère, 1576.

1576   *Livre de chansons nouvelles à cinc parties d'Orlande de Lassus.* Paris, A. Le Roy and R. Ballard, 1576.

1576   *Les Meslanges D'Orlande de Lassus.* Paris, A. Le Roy and R. Ballard, 1576.

1577^5 *Dixneufieme livre de chansons à quatre & cinq parties, d'Orlande de Lassus, & autres.* Paris, A. Le Roy and R. Ballard, 1577.

1577_6 *Zwey Bücher. Einer Neuen Kunstlichen Tabulatur auff Orgel und Instrument . . . Durch Bernhart Schmid.* Strasbourg, B. Jobin, 1577.

1577_7 *Musica de diversi autori la Bataglia Francese et canzon delli ucelli.* Venice, Ang. Gardano, 1577.

1578^{10} *Quatorzieme livre de chansons à quatre, & cinq parties d'Orlande de Lassus et autres.* Paris, A. Le Roy and R. Ballard, 1578.

1578^{11} *Quinzieme livre de chansons à quatre, cinq & six parties d'Orlande de Lassus & autres.* Paris, A. Le Roy and R. Ballard, 1578.

1578^{16} *Tiers livre de chansons a trois parties composé par Ad. Vuillart.* Paris, A. Le Roy and R. Ballard, 1578.

1578_3 *Obras de musica para tecla arpa y vihuela, de Antonio Cabeçon.* Madrid, F. Sanchez, 1578.

1578_4 *Renovata cythara: Hoc est Novi et commodissimi exercendae cytharae modi . . . Durch Sixt Kärgel.* Strasbourg, B. Jobin, 1578.

1578	*Second livre des Amours de P. de Ronsard . . . par Anthoine de Bertrand.* Paris, A. LeRoy and R. Ballard, 1578.
1579	*Musique de Guillaume Costeley.* Paris, A. Le Roy and R. Ballard, 1579.
1581[2]	*Dixneufieme livre de chansons à quatre & cinq parties, d'Orlande de Lassus, & autres.* Paris, A. Le Roy and R. Ballard, 1581.
1581	*Livre de chansons nouvelles à cinc parties d'Orlande de Lassus.* Paris, A. Le Roy and R. Ballard, 1581.
1582[1]	*Novae tabulae musicae testudinariae hexachordae et heptachordae Julii Caesaris Barbetti.* Strasbourg, B. Jobin, 1582.
1582[5]	*Hortulus Citharae vulgaris continens optimas fantasias, cantiones.* Antwerp, P. Phalèse and J. Bellère, 1582.
1583[6]	*Dousieme livre de chansons à quatre parties, d'Orlande de Lassus et autres.* Paris, A. Le Roy and R. Ballard, 1583.
1583[7]	*Vingdeuxieme livre de chansons à quatre & cinq parties, d'Orlande de Lassus et autres.* Paris, A. Le Roy and R. Ballard, 1583.
1583[8]	*Vingttroisieme livre de chansons à quatre & cinq parties, d'Orlande de Lassus et autres.* Paris, A. Le Roy and R. Ballard, 1583.
1584[2]	*Il vero modo di diminuir, con tutte le sorte di stromenti di fiato, . . . di Girolamo dalla Casa.* Venice, Ang. Gardane, 1584.
1584[6]	*Pratum musicum longe amoenissimum, cuius spatiosissimo, . . . Emanuelem Hadrianium.* Antwerp, P. Phalèse and R. Leon, 1584.
1585[11]	*Vingtdeuxieme livre de chansons à quatre & cinq parties, d'Orlande de Lassus et autres.* Paris, A. Le Roy and R. Ballard, 1585.
1585[12]	*Vingttroisieme livre de chansons à quatre & cinq parties, d'Orlande de Lassus et autres.* Paris, A. Le Roy and R. Ballard, 1585.
1586[6]	*Di Antonio Gardano il primo libro de canzoni francese a due voci, . . .* Venice, Ang. Gardano, 1586.
[1586][2]	*[Il Primo Libro d'Intavolatura d'arpicordo.]*
1586	*Les Meslanges D'Orlande de Lassus.* Paris, A. Le Roy and R. Ballard, 1586.
1586	*Meslanges de la Musique de Clau. Le Jeune.* Paris, A. Le Roy and R. Ballard, 1586.
1587[2]	*Quinzieme livre de chansons à quatre cinq & six parties. D'Orlande de Lassus et autres.* Paris, A. Le Roy and R. Ballard, 1587.
1587	*Meslanges de la Musique de Clau. Le Jeune.* Paris, A. Le Roy and R. Ballard, 1587.
1587	*Second livre des Amours de P. de Ronsard . . . par Anthoine de Bertrand.* Paris, A. Le Roy and R. Ballard, 1587.
1588[31]	*Canzon di diversi per sonar con ogni sorte di stromenti a quatro, cinque, et sei voci.* Venice, G. Vincenzi, 1588.
1589[5]	*Livre septieme des chansons a quatre parties.* Antwerp, P. Phalèse & J. Bellère, 1589.
1589[1]	*Orchesographie. et traicte en forme de dialogue, . . . apprendre & practiquer l'honneste exercise des dances . . . Par Thoinot arbeau.* Langres, 1589.
1591[4]	*Quatorzieme livre de chansons à quatre, a cinq parties d'Orlande de Lassus.* Paris, A. Le Roy, 1591.
1591[2]	*Motetti, madrigali et canzoni francese, di diversi . . . à Quattro, Cinque, & Sei Voci . . . da Giovanni Bassano.* Venice, G. Vincenti, 1591.

1591[3]   *Canzoni Francese Intavolate per sonar d'organo da Sperindio Bertoldo.* Venice, G. Vincenti, 1591.

1592[8]   *Livre septieme des chansons a quatre parties.* Antwerp, P. Phalèse & J. Bellère, 1592.

1592[6]   *Novum pratum musicum longe amoenissimum, cuius spatiosissimo, . . . Emanuelem Hadrianum.* Antwerp, P. Phalèse & J. Bellère, 1592.

1592[10] *Passaggi per potersi essercitare Nel diminuire terminatamente con ogni sorte d'instromenti . . . di Richardo Rogniono.* Venice, G. Vincenti, 1592.

1593[7]   *Di. Gio. Antonio Terzi da Bergamo, Intavolatura di Liutto.* Venice, R. Amadino, 1593.

1597[9]   *Livre septieme des chansons a quatre parties.* Antwerp, Vve J. Bellère, 1597.

1599[7]   *Intavolatura di liuto di Simone Molinaro Genovese Libro Primo.* Venice, R. Amadino, 1599.

1599[11] *Il secondo libro de intavolatura di Liuto di Gio. Antonio Terzi da Bergamo.* Venice, G. Vicenti, 1599.

1599   *Livre de chansons nouvelles à cinc parties d'Orlande de Lassus.* Paris, A. Le Roy and R. Ballard, 1599.

1601[4]   *Livre septieme des chansons vulgaires, de diverses autheurs à quatre parties.* Antwerp, P. Phalèse, 1601.

1605[5]   *Livre septieme des chansons vulgaires, de diverses autheurs à quatre parties.* Antwerp, P. Phalèse, 1605.

1608[11] *Livre septieme des chansons vulgaires, de diverses autheurs a quatre parties.* Amsterdam, C. Claessen, 1608.

1609[12] *Livre septieme des chansons vulgaires, de diverses auteurs a quatre parties.* Antwerp, P. Phalèse, 1609.

1613[7]   *Livre septieme des chansons vulgaires, de diverses auteurs a quatre parties.* Antwerp, P. Phalèse, 1613.

1617[6]   *Livre septiesme des chansons vulgaires de divers autheurs a quatre parties.* Douai, J. Bogart, 1617.

1617[6a] *Livre septieme des chansons vulgaires, de diverses autheurs a quatre parties.* Antwerp, P. Phalèse, 1617.

1632[5]   *Livre septieme des chansons vulgaires, de divers autheurs à quatre parties.* Amsterdam, J. Jansen, 1632.

1633[2]   *Livre septiesme des chansons vulgaires de divers autheurs a quatre parties.* Douai, P. Bogart, 1633.

1640[6]   *Livre septieme des chansons vulgaires, de diverses autheurs a quatre parties.* Amsterdam, B. Jansz, 1640.

1644[3]   *Livre septieme, dat is, het boek vande zanghkunst.* Amsterdam, J. Jansen, 1644.